献给九十华诞的黄华同志
Dedicated to Huang Hua on His 90th Birthday

筹备单位

中 国 福 利 会
中 国 宋 庆 龄 基 金 会
中 国 国 际 友 好 联 络 会
中 国 国 际 友 人 研 究 会
中 国 长 城 学 会

SPONSORED AND PREPARED BY

China Welfare Institute
China Soong Ching Ling Foundation
China Association for International Friendly Contact
China Society for People's Friendship Studies
Great Wall Society of China

2003 年 8 月　　第 1 版
August 2003　　First Edition
2006 年 12 月　　第 2 版
December 2006　　Second Edition

黄华

年逾九十题

前　　言

我和黄华同志是同一时代的人，从年轻时就一直追随着中国共产党，我们的经历和党的战斗历程密切相连。光阴荏苒，如今我们已是耄耋之年。看到中国经济蓬勃发展，人民生活不断改善，国际地位与日俱增，心里感到十分欣慰。

我与黄华同志相识在一二·九运动时期。他在燕京，我在清华，都是风华正茂、抗日爱国的热血青年。我们不甘做亡国奴，和北平、天津的学生们一道高举抗日救国的旗帜，和反动军警顽强斗争。中国共产党领导中国工农红军在陕北建立的革命根据地，如同光辉的朝阳吸引着成千上万爱国志士，我们也投笔从戎，奔向延安。

1946年的一件趣事令我至今记忆犹新。那时我在南京梅园新村周恩来副主席处工作，黄华在北平军事调处执行部工作。中央委托他从北平专程捎一百锭黄金给梅园新村作经费。赖祖烈同志点过后开玩笑说："不对呀，怎么多出一锭？"黄华听了诙谐地说："噢，是生了小金锭了。"

黄华从事外事工作数十年。在陕北保安，他为埃德加·斯诺做翻译，到延安后又接待过许多外国朋友和记者，包括美军观察组等。建国后他调入外交部，在周总理和陈毅同志的直接领导下，多次参加新中国重大外交活动，从而培养了作为外交官必须具备的胆略、气魄和斗争艺术。黄华同志深受周总理高风亮节、庄重洒脱的外交风范影响，牢记周总理"外事工作，授权有限"的八字告诫，谦虚谨慎，成为一名立场坚定，掌握政策，钻研业务，开拓进取的外交家。

记得在1989年5月底，正是北京发生那场政治风波前夕，黄华要去美国出席国际行动理事会。行前，他坚守党的外事纪律，通过姚依林找我研究中央的对外口径。在中国革命艰难、漫长的道路上，黄华始终站稳革命立场，和党中央保持一致。

黄华不仅不忘为中国革命和建设倾注过心血的国际友人，而且非常重视结交新朋友。无论过去、现在和将来，我们都需要各国人民的支持和帮助。他领导的几个民间组织，在增进与外国人民的了解和友谊方面做了许多工作。

黄华同志年届九十，几个民间友好团体筹划出一本纪念性的画册，我很赞同。从那些弥足珍贵的照片中，我们可以看到他几十年走过的光荣岁月。

宋平

2002年8月

编者注：宋平是中国共产党第十三、十四届中央委员会政治局常委。

FOREWORD

Comrade Huang Hua and I are contemporaries. From the days of our youth, we have always followed the Communist Party of China (CPC). Our lives have been closely related to its struggles. Time has slipped by, and now we are old. We are gratified to see that China's economy is flourishing, the people's livelihood is improving steadily, and China's international status continues to rise.

I met Comrade Huang Hua during the December 9th Student Movement of 1935, when we were university students, he at Yenching (Peking), I at Tsinghua. Ardently patriotic, we strongly opposed Japanese aggression, determined that China would never be enslaved. Together with students from Beiping (Beijing) and Tianjin, we held high the banner of resistance against Japan and for national salvation, and fought tenaciously against the reactionary government's troops and police.

The Chinese Workers and Peasants Red Army, led by the CPC, established a revolutionary base in northern Shaanxi Province. Like a brilliant rising red sun it fascinated tens of thousands of noble-minded patriots. Huang Hua and I cast aside our pens and hurried to join the revolutionary forces in Yan'an.

An amusing incident still remains with me. In 1946 I was working for Vice-Chairman Zhou Enlai at Meiyuan New Village in the city of Nanjing. Huang Hua was in Beiping (Beijing) with the Military Executive Headquarters. The Central Command entrusted him with a mission to deliver 100 ingots of gold to Meiyuan New Village. Comrade Lai Zulie first checked them over." How come there is one ingot too many?" he joked. " They must have given birth to a little one!" Huang Hua rejoined, straight-faced.

He was involved in foreign affairs for several decades, starting in the thirties in Bao'an in northern Shaanxi Province when he acted as interpreter for Edgar Snow. Later, in Yan'an he met with quite a few foreign friends and journalists, as well as members of the U.S. Military Observer Group (popularly known as the " Dixie Mission") .

After the founding of the People's Republic of China in 1949, Huang Hua was appointed to the Ministry of Foreign Affairs. Under the direct leadership of Premier Zhou Enlai and Foreign Minister Chen Yi, he took part in many important diplomatic activities. These developed in him the boldness of vision and maneuvering talents so essential to a skilled diplomat.

Deeply influenced by Zhou Enlai's highly principled conduct in matters of diplomacy, his serious yet relaxed charm, Huang Hua bore always in mind the Premier's caution: " There is a limit to how much you can concede in foreign affairs." Huang Hua was a modest and prudent diplomat, a man of steadfast principle with a firm grasp of policy, a thorough professional of pioneering and enterprising spirit.

I remember the end of May 1989, just before the outbreak of the political storm which followed in June. Huang Hua was about to leave for the U.S. to attend a meeting of the Inter-Action Council. In strict observance of Party discipline, through Yao Yilin he checked with me on the stance of the Central Committee regarding this complicated situation. On New China's long and difficult road, whenever the revolution hit a snag, Huang Hua stood rock-solid with the Communist Party Central Committee.

In addition to always remembering the foreign friends who poured their energies into China's revolution and construction, Huang Hua devotes considerable attention to making new friends. Whether past, present or future, China needs the support and help of friends abroad. Several NGOs under Huang Hua's leadership have done much to promote international people's friendship and understanding.

Comrade Huang Hua has attained the age of ninety. Five of the NGOs — the China Welfare Institute, the Soong Ching Ling Foundation, the China Association for International Friendly Contact, the China Society for People's Friendship Studies and the Great Wall Society of China —— plan to publish a pictorial album commemorating him. I heartily approve this idea. The precious photos it contains will serve to recall to us the splendid achievements of Huang Hua's many years.

Song Ping
August 2002

Editor's note: Song Ping, a member of the Standing Committee of the Political Bureau of the 13th, 14th CPC Central Committee.

序　言

我所认识的黄华同志

　　我同黄华同志相识是在抗日战争后期，在延安外事组工作时。当时的印象是：他是一位表情严肃，不苟言笑，对工作十分认真和勤恳的领导。

　　黄华是新中国许多重大外交事件的历史见证人和参与者。1935年一二·九北平学生运动，他是领导人之一，同美国记者埃德加·斯诺夫妇相熟与友好。1936年夏，黄华陪伴斯诺在陕北保安和西部前线采访中央领导人和红军将士。1937年初，在延安接待史沫特莱、海伦·斯诺、贝特兰等友人。1944年美军观察组到延安常驻，1946年北平军事调处执行部成立，他同美国官方有不少交道。

　　1949年4月，奉周恩来副主席的指示，黄华从天津调任南京军管会外事处长，以私人身份与当时留在南京的前美国驻华大使司徒雷登建立接触。1953年朝鲜停战后，他作为中国人民志愿军谈判代表团成员在板门店参加中朝方面同美韩代表讨论政治解决的谈判。

　　他在担任驻加纳和阿联（埃及）大使时，访问了多哥、达荷美、坦桑尼亚、毛里求斯、刚果（布）等非洲国家，接触了许多非洲国家和民族解放运动的领导人，为增进了解、推动建交作出了成就。

　　中美关系始终是我国外交工作的重点。1971年7月，黄华参加接待秘密来访的美国总统国家安全助理基辛格。随着中美关系解冻，双方在1978年底正式建立外交关系。建交时遗留的美国售台武器问题继续困扰着两国关系。经过两国代表持续、耐心和字斟句酌的谈判，最后于1982年发表了《八一七公报》。《八一七公报》同《上海公报》一起，都是中美关系中里程碑式的文件，严格遵循，认真执行，一定会促进两国关系不断发展。

　　1971年10月，联合国恢复我国的合法权利，中国开始全面进入多边外交领域。黄华担任首任常驻联合国组织和安全理事会代表。联合国讨论的议题广泛，各方面关系复杂，现场交锋多，政治影响大。因此，做好联合国工作，决非易事。黄华领导下的代表团遵照毛泽东主席和周恩来总理的指示，对联合国加深调查研究，勤奋努力，逐步克服了初期情况不熟、经验不足的困难，较好地执行了中央的方针政策。值得一提的是，我代表团于1972年初向非殖民地化委员会提出，要求将香港、澳门从殖民地名单中删除。委员会接受这项建议并将其载入向联合国大会的报告，联合国大会以压倒多数票予以通过，这就为杜绝香港、澳门问题的复杂化，为我国日后收回香港、澳门主权的谈判工作打了重要的前哨仗。

随着改革开放形势的发展，我国对联合国的看法也更加深入和全面。在他担任外长期间，我国参加了联合国的裁军和人权会议；接受多边援助；建立同联合国开发计划署、世界银行、国际货币基金组织的合作；有区别地参加联合国维和行动等等。多边外交局面有了新的开展。

中央一直关心我国同北方邻国苏联的关系。黄华外长及时建议举行中苏副外长级定期会谈，交换意见，以促进两国关系。此后他于1982年11月以中国政府特使身份参加勃列日涅夫葬礼时，进一步向苏联新领导人转达了中国领导人关于共同努力使两国关系逐步恢复正常的愿望。这在两国人民中产生了良好反应。

中国和日本是一衣带水的邻邦，中日友好是两国人民的共同愿望，是邓小平同志紧抓的大事。黄华外长同外交部的同志们积极进行中日和平友好条约的谈判，经过不少曲折，条约终于在1978年8月签订，并在东京举行批准书的交换仪式。邓小平副总理亲自出席，以示我国的重视。

1972年2月，中国的老朋友埃德加·斯诺病情危重，周总理急电给在亚的斯亚贝巴出席安理会会议的黄华，要他赶赴瑞士探望，传达毛主席、周总理的关切和问候。马海德大夫已率领医疗组在那里看护治疗。当这三个老朋友见面时，三双手紧握在一起，斯诺兴奋而诙谐地说："三个赤匪又聚在一起了。"斯诺满脸笑容，一瞬间充分流露出他从对中国、对老朋友们三十多年结下的深情厚谊中所感到的由衷的高兴与眷恋。

由于黄华同众多友好人士交往的这种"特点"，在他退出第一线后，仍然有很多外国朋友找他，他仍然积极活跃在民间外交和社会活动的舞台上。他经推选担任宋庆龄基金会、中国福利会、中国国际友好联络会、长城学会等很多社团的领导人，并作为知名人士应邀参加国际行动理事会（由三十多位离职各国政要组成）。他亲自组建的中国国际友人研究会，与许多外国民间团体进行友好交流活动。

今天，九旬高龄的黄华依旧每天阅读书报，关心国内外大事，不时接待来访的外国朋友，并且经常上网看时论，查资料，不忘"与时俱进"。勤耕耘，广交友，应该是外交界的一个好传统吧！

现在，《黄华》画册出版了。图片从一个侧面展示一个革命知识青年在党的指引和培育下成长的过程。我希望读者会喜爱这本书，希望广大干部和青年可以从中得到鼓舞和激励。

凌青

2002 年 8 月

编者注：凌青曾任中共中央延安外事组成员，常驻联合国和安理会代表、驻委内瑞拉共和国大使，现任中国国际友人研究会会长。

PREFACE

THE HUANG HUA I KNOW

I met Huang Hua near the end of the War Against Japanese Aggression, when I was working in the Foreign Affairs Group in Yan'an. He impressed me as a rather solemn, reserved person who took his leadership responsibilities very seriously.

Huang Hua witnessed and participated in many important events in New China's history. He was one of the leaders of the Beiping student movement of December 9, 1935. He was a good friend of American journalist Edgar Snow and his wife Helen Foster (who wrote under the name " Nym Wales"). In the summer of 1936, when Snow interviewed Communist leaders in Bao'an in northern Shaanxi, and generals and troops at the western front, Huang Hua acted as his interpreter. In early 1937, in Yan'an, he looked after American friends Agnes Smedley, Nym Wales and James Bertram. A U.S. Military Observer Group set up in Yan'an in 1944, followed in 1946 by the Military Executive Headquarters established in Beiping (Beijing), brought Huang Hua into frequent contact with American officials.

In April 1949, Vice-Chairman Zhou Enlai ordered him transferred from Tianjin to Nanjing to assume the post of director of the Foreign Affairs Division of the Military Control Commission. Former U. S. Ambassador Leighton Stuart was then still in Nanjing, and Huang Hua established contact with him in a private capacity.

After the Korean War ended in 1953, Huang Hua, as a member of the negotiating team of the Chinese People's Volunteers on the Sino-North Korean side, took part at Panmunjom in the discussions with the U.S. - South Korean side regarding a political settlement of the conflict.

While serving as Ambassador to Ghana and the United Arab Republic (Egypt), he visited Togo, Dahomey (Benin), Tanzania, Mauritius and Congo (Brazzaville). He also met with leaders of many African countries and national liberation movements, promoting understanding and hastening the establishment of diplomatic relations.

Sino-U.S. relations have always been a focal point of our diplomacy. In July of 1971, Huang Hua took part in receiving the American envoy Dr. Kissinger who had been sent secretly to arrange a meeting between President Richard Nixon and Chairman Mao Zedong. Nixon's visit to China marked a thaw in Sino - U.S. relations, culminating in the establishment of formal diplomatic ties at the end of 1978.

The sale of U.S. arms to Taiwan continues to disturb Sino - U.S. amity. After sustained and patient negotiations, weighing every word, both sides finally signed the "August 17 Communique" in 1982, another milestone document in Sino-U.S. relations. Strict adherence to these documents and their earnest implementation will certainly enhance relations between the two countries.

In October 1971, the United Nations restored China's legitimate rights, and we began full participation in many-faceted foreign diplomacy. Huang Hua was China's first permanent representative to the UN and the Security Council. The UN discusses a broad range of complicated issues, with frequent on-the-spot confrontations, exercising a tremendous political influence. Being a UN representative is no easy matter. The Chinese delegation which Huang Hua headed, acting in accordance with instructions from Chairman Mao Zedong and Premier Zhou Enlai, studied the UN intensely. It gradually overcame its unfamiliarity and acquired sufficient experience to be able to meet the requirements of China's government.

For example, the Chinese delegation early in 1972 proposed to the Decolonization Committee that it exclude Hong Kong and Macao from its list of colonies. The Committee accepted the proposal and submitted it in a report to the General Assembly, which then adopted it by an overwhelming majority. This assured there would be no complications regarding the status of Hong Kong and Macao, and cleared away any obstacle to restoration of our sovereignty over them.

As China intensified reform and opening up, we expanded our participation in the UN. After Huang Hua became Foreign Minister (1976~1982), China took part in UN conferences on disarmament and human rights, accepted multilateral assistance, cooperated with the UN Development Program, the World Bank, and the IMF, and participated in UN peace-keeping activities. Our multilateral diplomacy entered a new stage.

China has always been deeply concerned about relations with our northern neighbor, the former Soviet Union. As Foreign Minister, Huang Hua proposed a regular exchange of views, at a deputy foreign minister level, to promote bilateral relations. In November 1982, when he attended the funeral of Soviet President Leonid Brezhnev as China's special envoy, he conveyed to the new Soviet leadership the hope of China's leaders that mutual efforts be made to gradually normalize relations. This evoked a favorable response from the peoples of both countries.

China and Japan are separated only by a strip of water. Friendship is the desire of both peoples. Huang Hua and his colleagues in China's Ministry of Foreign Affairs conducted long and difficult negotiations with Japan aiming at a Sino-Japanese Treaty of Peace and Friendship. It was finally signed in August 1978 with a ceremonial exchange of instruments of ratification in Tokyo. Vice-Premier Deng Xiaoping attended personally, as a mark of the importance China attached to good relations with Japan.

In February 1972, China's old friend Edgar Snow was dying of cancer in Switzerland. Premier Zhou Enlai sent an urgent cable to Huang Hua who was attending a meeting of the Security Council in Addis Abeba, directing him to hurry to Switzerland and convey to Snow his deep concern and that of Chairman Mao Zedong. A Chinese medical group under Dr. George Hatem (Ma Haide) was already in attendance. When the three old friends met, they tightly clasped hands. Snow, very moved, clearly reflected how he cherished their friendship of more than thirty years: " The three'Red Bandits' are together again!"Snow said with a warm smile.

Because Huang Hua enjoyed an intimate relationship with innumerable foreign friends, many continued to seek him out after he officially retired. He is still active in people-to-people diplomacy and on the stage of public affairs. He has been elected president of several mass organizations such as the Soong Ching Ling Foundation, the China Welfare Institute, the China Association for International Friendly Contact, and the Great Wall Society of China. He has also been invited to join the Inter-Action Council — an international body of some thirty prominent figures from various countries who have retired from public office. The China Society for People's Friendship Studies, which he personally set up, has been engaged in friendly exchanges with many foreign people's organizations.

Today, at the age of ninety, Huang Hua still reads the daily newspapers, is concerned about major domestic and international events, and continues to receive visitors from abroad. In step with the times, he daily peruses current affairs articles and checks reference material on his computer. A large circle of friends and hard work is an old tradition in the diplomatic community!

The pictorial album HUANG HUA is off the press. It shows one aspect of how a young student developed into a mature revolutionary under the guidance and teaching of the Chinese Communist Party. I hope that all readers will enjoy it, and that it will provide inspiration and encouragement to China's many civil service workers and youth.

Ling Qing
August 2002

Editor's note: Ling Qing was a member of Foreign Affairs Group in Yan'an, Permanent Representative to UN and Security Council, Ambassador to Venezuela, and is currently president of China Society for People's Friendship Studies.

GREETINGS

HUANG HUA — My Friend

Huang Hua is 90 but, after 70 years, has preserved the youthfulness of his early 20s as a leading activist of the historic Beijing student movement of December 1935 that helped arouse all China to resist the spreading threat of Japanese militarist aggression that menaced her national existence.

To that time, too, belong the earliest roots of the future diplomatic career that, after the Liberation, would take him to the post of Minister of Foreign Affairs of the People's Republic of China. Fluent in English, he was a link of the student movement with staunch foreign friends like the Americans Edgar and Helen Snow and the New Zealand author James Bertram, his fellow alumnus and room-mate at Yenching (Yanjing) University. Later he would be Snow's interpreter on the latter's window-opening journey which would result in the world-famous book *Red Star Over China*. And Bertram, on the basis of personal travels, would also write reliable and valuable books on the Xi'an Incident of 1936, and on the areas led by the Chinese Communist Party, where like Snow he interviewed Mao Zedong, and was an eyewitness to their earliest fruitful development of guerrilla and mobile war against Japanese occupation.

I myself, though I already knew of Huang Hua from the Snows, first met him some 60 years ago, in Yan'an in 1944, when as secretary to Zhu De, commander-in-chief of China's Communist-led armies, he acted his interpreter in a separate interview I had with that world-famous revolutionary warrior. I was in Yan'an as part of the first press group to visit there after five years of tight news-blockade by the Chiang Kai-shek government, finally broken by the persistent efforts of foreign newsmen plus the pressure of China's allies for Japan's final defeat at a time when the Chiang regime had virtually ceased to resist the Japanese aggressors within China.

Our next contact was seven crucial years later, in the young People's Republic of China, in Shanghai where Huang Hua was in charge of the liberated city's foreign affairs. My late wife Elsie Cholmeley and I, newly arrived from some years in the United States on the invitation of Soong Ching Ling (Mme. Sun Yat-sen) were preparing the printing at that time there, of the new magazine *China Reconstructs* (now renamed *China Today*). Huang Hua presided at a welcoming reception for us. Also attending were staff members of *Shanghai News,* a newly established English language daily in the city.

Since that time Huang Hua has had a far-reaching and varied diplomatic career. After attending the epoch-making Bandung Conference in 1955, he became China's first ambassador to Ghana, West Africa and special envoy to several African countries that had shaken off colonial control, and after new China's restoration to her rightful place in the United Nations, with the acclaiming votes of the newly independent states of the Third World, he became his country's first permanent representative in the world body. Since retirement as Foreign Minister he has been regularly participating in the international gatherings of retired statesmen known as the Inter-Action Council.

Within the past 20 years now, I have had the pleasure and honor of working with Huang Hua in several organizations which he has headed the Smedley-Strong-Snow Society of China (later renamed the China Society for People's Friendship Studies), the China Welfare Institute and the Soong Ching Ling Foundation. He is devoted to the memory and heritage of Soong Ching Ling as a principled revolutionary, a pioneer of modernization and a builder of bridges between forward-looking and peace-loving people everywhere.

I am proud that he has often called me his friend.

I. Epstein

December 2002

Editor's note: Israel Epstein, born in 1915 in Poland, settled in Tianjin in 1920 and was engaged in journalism from his teenage years. He sympathizes and supports the revolutionary struggle of Chinese people. In 1938 he was a member of the Central Committee of the China Defence League established by Soong Ching Ling in Hong Kong. After the founding of New China, he joined and helped to found the magazine *China Reconstructs* (now renamed *China Today*), of which he rose to be chief editor. He became a Chinese citizen and is currently a member of the Standing Committee of the Chinese People's Political Consultative Conference National Committee, vice-chairman of China Welfare Institute and Soong Ching Ling Foundation and vice-president of the China Society for People's Friendship Studies.

我的朋友 —— 黄华

　　黄华九十岁了，但他仍保持着他七十年前的那种青年气息。1935年12月，他二十岁刚出头，北平发生了历史性的学生运动，他是参与领导这场学生运动的积极分子。那时在日本加强军国主义的威胁下，中国处于危急存亡之秋，学生运动唤起全中国人民起来抵抗日本的侵略。

　　他那时候从事的活动成了他后来外交生涯的基础。全国解放后，他被派到中华人民共和国外交部工作。他讲一口流利的英语，他与那些对中国革命坚信不疑的朋友，如美国的埃德加·斯诺和海伦·斯诺，新西兰的作家、他在燕京大学时的同学、室友詹姆斯·贝特兰建立了联系。往后，他在斯诺那次向世界报道中国红色区域的旅行中做了斯诺的翻译，结果是斯诺写成了享誉世界的《西行漫记》一书。贝特兰根据个人旅行见闻，也写了关于1936年西安事变和中国共产党领导的地区的一些材料可靠、有价值的书籍。他和斯诺一样，采访过毛泽东，也是一位亲眼看到共产党领导下的人民利用游击战、运动战抵抗日本占领取得初期成效的见证人。

　　我自己虽早就从斯诺夫妇那里知道黄华，但第一次见他是在大约六十年前，1944年在延安，他是中国共产党所领导的军队的总司令朱德的秘书，我个别采访这位世界著名的战士时，他担任翻译。那一年我到延安，是打破了蒋介石政权严密封锁新闻达五年之久去的第一个访问延安的记者代表团成员，这是由于中外记者的不断努力和中国的盟国一定要彻底击败日本而施加压力的结果，那时蒋政权实际上已停止了在中国国内抵抗日本侵略者。

　　我们下一次接触是在经历了严酷斗争的七年以后，在年轻的中华人民共和国刚刚建立时，黄华负责解放了的上海的外事工作。我和我已过世的妻子邱茉莉在美国待了几年以后，应宋庆龄（孙中山夫人）的邀请，参与她筹办一本新杂志《中国建设》（现更名为《今日中国》）的工作。黄华主持一个欢迎我们的招待会，上海新出版的英文报纸《上海新闻》社的职工也出席招待会了。

　　自那以后，黄华度过了多年远涉重洋、执行多种任务的外交生涯。1955年出席划时代的万隆会议后，他成为中国派往刚摆脱了殖民控制的非洲和阿拉伯国家的首任大使。1971年，经过第三世界独立国家的支持，联合国恢复了新中国的合法席位，他成了这个世界机构中的中国首任常驻代表。从外交部长的岗位上退下来后，他经常出席一些前国家领导人的国际集会，如国际行动理事会。

　　二十多年来，我很愉快和荣幸地在以他为首的几个民间团体中同他一道工作，如史沫特莱、斯特朗、斯诺学会（后改名为中国国际友人研究会）、中国福利会和宋庆龄基金会。宋庆龄是一位有原则的革命家、现代化的先驱和在有远见卓识及热爱和平的人民之间架设桥梁的人，黄华致力于继承和发扬光大她的遗志。

　　他常说我是他的朋友，我为此感到自豪。

爱泼斯坦
2002 年 12 月

　　编者注：伊斯雷尔·爱泼斯坦1915年生于波兰。1920年定居天津，青年时即从事新闻工作。同情和支持中国人民的革命斗争。1938年他担任宋庆龄在香港创建的保卫中国同盟的中央委员。新中国成立后参加《中国建设》（现改名为《今日中国》）杂志的创办，曾担任总编辑。他加入了中国国籍，曾担任全国政协常务委员以及中国福利会、宋庆龄基金会副主席和中国国际友人研究会的副会长。

目　　录

CONTENTS

第一部分

积极投入北平学生抗日救亡运动
到陕北参加红军
（1935～1937）

　　1931年爆发九一八事件，日本帝国主义大举武装侵略，占领了中国东北三省。蒋介石执行对外投降，对内反共内战的政策，命令二十余万东北军撤至长城以南。当时在锦州东北交通大学求学的黄华（原名王汝梅）与大批同学愤然离开东北，来到北平。次年考入燕京大学。日本的侵略野心绝不止是东北，而是吞并全中国！1935年5月，《何梅协定》签订后，蒋、日政府策划华北五省自治，成立"冀察政务委员会"傀儡政府。华北大片土地包括北平和天津即将成为日本的殖民地，华北人民眼看要成为亡国奴。

　　当时，中国共产党领导下的地下组织——北平学联——决定发动平津各校抗日大游行。12月8日，时为燕大学生会执委会主席的黄华同燕大学生会主席张兆林召开大会提议参加次日大游行，得到全体学生坚决响应，于是爆发要求抗日救亡的一二·九运动。一二·九运动迅速成为全国性运动。

　　黄华在1936年初参加了中国共产党。

　　1936年6月中旬，黄华应美国记者埃德加·斯诺的要求，为他担任采访陕北苏区的翻译，秘密离开北平。同年10月，斯诺离开保安回北平写书。黄华参加红军。

　　1937年1月，红军进驻延安。黄华随军进城。

Part One

**Active participation in the Beiping (Beijing) student movement
of resistance against Japan and for national salvation and
going to northern Shaanxi to join the Red Army
(1935~1937)**

With the outbreak of the September 18th Incident in 1931, the Japanese imperialists carried out armed aggression on a large scale, and seized China's three northeastern provinces. Chiang Kai-shek implemented a policy of capitulation in foreign affairs and anti-Communist civil war at home, and ordered the Northeastern Army of over 200,000 troops to withdraw to the south of the Great Wall. At that time, Huang Hua (original name: Wang Rumei) who was studying at Northeast Jiaotong University in Jinzhou, left the Northeast in anger for Beiping (Beijing) together with large numbers of fellow students. He was admitted to Yenching University in the following year. Japan's aggressive ambitions were not limited to the Northeast only, but sought to swallow up the whole of China. After the signing of the "Ho-Umezu Agreement" in May 1935, the governments of Chiang Kai-shek and Japan plotted autonomy in the five provinces of northern China, and set up a puppet regime of "Political Council for Hopei (Hebei) and Chahar". A vast area of northern China, including Beiping and Tianjin, would soon become a Japanese colony. People in this region would be turned into slaves of a foreign country.

The Beiping Student Union, an underground organization led by the Communist Party of China, decided to mobilize students of Beiping and Tianjin to stage an anti-Japanese demonstration. On December 8, Huang Hua, then chairman of executive committee, and Zhang Zhaolin, president of Yenching University Student Union, convened a meeting, proposing to join the demonstration the following day, which won firm response from all the students. The December 9th Movement which was then launched to demand resistance against Japan and for national salvation, became a nation-wide campaign.

Huang Hua joined the Communist Party of China early in 1936.

In mid-June 1936, Huang Hua, at the request of American journalist Edgar Snow, undertook to be his interpreter on his visit to Chinese Soviet Areas in northern Shaanxi. Huang Hua left Beiping in secret. In October, Snow left Bao'an and returned to Beiping to write his book. Huang Hua joined the Red Army.

In January 1937, Huang Hua followed with the Red Army, which moved to Yan'an.

I-1　黄华于1932年考入燕京大学。照片为好友、同校新闻系学生张兆林于1935年所摄。

I-1 Huang Hua is admitted to Yenching University in 1932. Photo taken in 1935 by his good friend Zhang Zhaolin, a journalism major.

I-2　黄华，原名王汝梅，1913年生于河北省磁县。1926年就读磁县中学。父亲王浩然，曾任县里的督学。图为原磁县中学近貌。

I-2 Huang Hua (original name: Wang Rumei), born in Cixian county of Hebei Province in 1913, goes to county high school in 1926. His father is the county educational inspector. The present school building.

16

I-3　燕京大学参加一二·九学生运动的部分领导骨干。左一为陈翰伯，左三为龚澎，左四为黄华，正中为张兆林，右二为赵荣声，右三为龚普生。

Some key members from Yenching University taking part in December 9th Student Movement. First left: Chen Hanbo, third left: Gong Peng, fourth left: Huang Hua, center: Zhang Zhaolin, second right: Zhao Rongsheng, third right: Gong Pusheng.

I-4　1935年12月9日清晨，燕京大学五百五十多名学生结队离校向北平城进发。他们高呼"打倒日本帝国主义！""反对华北'自治'！"

Early morning December 9, 1935. Over 550 Yenching University students gather to march to Beiping City, shouting slogans "Down with Japanese imperialism!" "Oppose 'autonomy' of North China!"

I-5 燕京、清华和城郊的几所大、中学校学生的游行队伍被紧闭各城门的军警挡在西直门外。

The procession of students from Tsinghua, Yenching and other universities and middle schools in the outskirts of Beiping is blocked outside Xizhimen by Kuomintang soldiers and policemen at closed city gate.

I-6 近两千名愤怒的学生在北平西直门外举行群众大会。张兆林、陆璀、赵志萱等许多人轮流用喇叭筒讲演，慷慨激昂。照片中持喇叭者为清华大学的陆璀，其右是燕京大学的张兆林。

About 2,000 angry students hold a mass rally outside Xizhimen. Lu Cui from Tsinghua University (holding trumpet), Zhang Zhaolin on her right.

I-7　一二·九之后，各校学生根据宋庆龄女士关于行动起来的建议，积极准备南下向工人、农民和城镇市民扩大抗日宣传。图为1936年1月燕京大学学生在校园内集会。右一为黄华。
After December 9, students on Soong Ching Ling's recommendation, prepare to go south to spread anti-Japanese propaganda among workers, peasants and townspeople. Students hold a rally on Yenching University campus in January 1936. First right: Huang Hua.

I-8　南下扩大宣传团第三团第二大队（燕京大学）第三小队合影。右一为黄华。
A propaganda team of Yenching University.First right:Huang Hua.

I-9 1936年1月15日，南下扩大宣传团第三团（即燕京清华队）在离北平八十公里的高碑店与大队特务警察发生冲突，彻夜对峙。次日晨，同学们用英语讨论决定：一、全体返校；二、成立组织，继续抗日救亡。图中间为燕京、清华同学，两边是特务警察。

January 15, 1936. At Gaobeidian, 80 km from Beiping, a propaganda team of Yenching and Tsinghua students in conflict with secret agents and policemen. The following morning, students after discussions in English decide to return to school and set up an organization. Students encircled by secret agents and policemen.

内六區署謹將解往綏靖公署監獄學生花名列後

姓名　年歲　籍貫　某捉學生性別備

吳志洙　二〇　綏遠　志成　仝
張作華　二四　廣東　仝　仝
任澤雨　二一　四川　仝　仝
鄧維熙　二一　江西清華　仝
柯家龍　二二　廣東燕大　仝
岳成武　一八　安徽大同　仝
梁德興　二三　廣東清華　仝
謝雲暉　二四　四川　仝
葉妃霖　二二　湖北北大　男生
李鼎聲　二二　河北清華　仝
烏義榮　一七　山東大同　仝
盧英石　二二　安徽清華　仝
蔡承祖　二〇　江蘇清華　仝
魏戈的　二二　河南弘達　仝
于壯生　二一　仝大同　仝
王汝梅　二二　河北燕大　仝
張肇敏　二二　山西清華　仝
朱和同　二四　湖北清華　仝
裴奎山　二五　山西仝華　仝
羅邪瑛　二一　仝滙文　仝

I-10

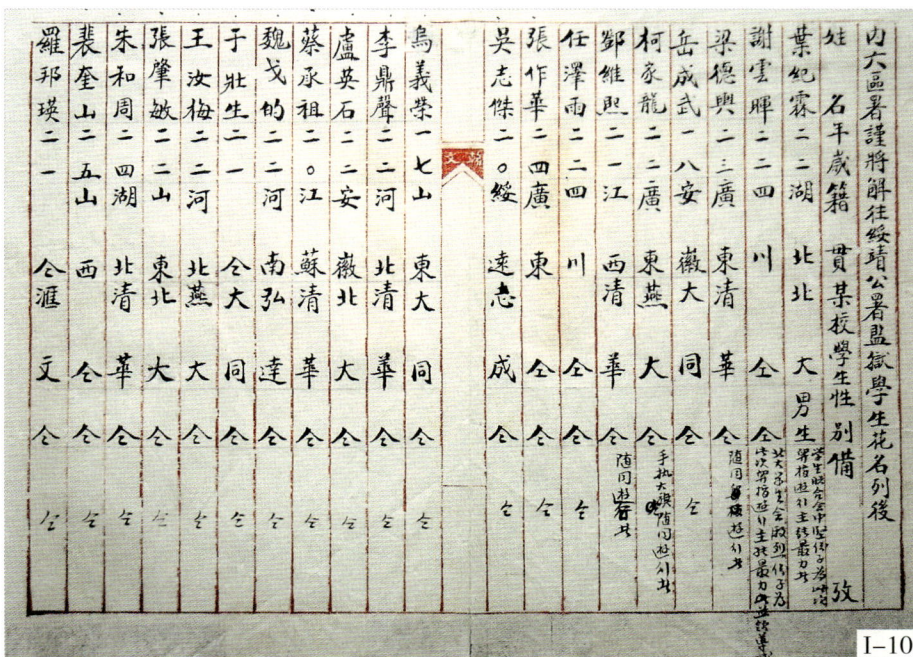

I-10 1936年3月31日，北平的大中学生为监狱中牺牲的学生抬棺游行，被军警冲散。黄华被捕，上了脚镣，关押在陆军监狱。半个多月后被学校师生营救出狱。图为监狱的部分被捕者名单。左五为王汝梅（黄华）。

March 31, 1936. Beiping students hold a demonstration carrying a coffin of the student who died in prison. Huang Hua is arrested and put into prison with feet in fetters. The list of part of students in prison. The name of Wang Rumei (Huang Hua) is fifth from left.

I-12

I-12 1936年6月初，黄华依靠吴雷川奖学金读完燕京大学经济系二、三、四年级课程。图为毕业前夕的留影。6月中旬，应燕大新闻系讲师埃德加·斯诺之邀，秘密离开北平，赴陕北保安为其担任翻译。

Early June 1936. Huang Hua finishes studies in economics at Yenching University on scholarship. Photo shows him shortly before graduation. In mid-June, he goes to Bao'an in northern Shaanxi, on Edgar Snow's request to act as his interpreter.

《牢狱之花》诗一首

野性的呼唤

我企望那殷红的血迹，
那血迹是为战斗而洒的。
我渴慕那野性的呼唤，
那呼唤是为了 450000000 啊！

我看见那辽远的信号了，
我听见那粗壮的咆哮了，
虽然镣铐锁住两脚，
心还是奔驰的啊！

I-11

I-11 1936年4月，黄华在监狱中主编了几期名为《牢狱之花》的手抄小报。图为燕京大学难友根据记忆记录的一首佚名诗。

April 1936. Huang Hua edits in prison some handwritten tabloids. A poem written by an inmate and carried in the tabloid.

An Unruly Call

I seek for the dark red blood,
Which is shed for the struggle.
I yearn for the unruly call,
Which is for the sake of 450 million people.

I saw the distant signal,
And heard the deep resonant roar.
Though my feet are in fetters,
Yet my heart is still seething with excitement.

I-13　1936年8月，斯诺在保安采访参加长征的老革命徐特立（左一），左二为黄华，右一为斯诺。因黄华可能被派到白区工作，斯诺根据黄华的要求，不给他拍照，不提他的名字，斯诺在《西行漫记》中信守诺言。图片为红军干部所摄。

August 1936. Photo taken by a Red Army cadre shows Snow (first right) interviewing Xu Teli (first left), an old revolutionary of the Long March. Because Huang Hua could be sent to work in white areas, in compliance with Huang Hua's request, Snow does not take a picture of Huang Hua, nor mentions him in the book *Red Star Over China*. Second left: Huang Hua.

I-14

I-14 受斯诺采访陕北的影响，燕京大学学生于1937年4月组团访问延安，他们中许多是中共秘密党员。前排自左至右为：柯华、王向立、赵荣声、陈龙、欧阳方,第二排自左至右为：张非垢、靳明、李质清、郑怀之、朱邵天，后排右一为黄华。

April 1937. Influenced by Snow's visit to northern Shaanxi, Yenching University students organize a group to visit Yan'an. Many of them are secret Communist Party members. From left in second row: Zhang Feigou,Jin Ming,Li Zhiqing,Zheng Huaizhi,Zhu Shaotian.First right in back row:Huang Hua.

第二部分

在延安从事党的早期外事工作

（1944～1947）

四十年代初，黄华被调任朱德总司令的政治秘书。

1944年6月，在中外记者的强烈要求下，国民党政府允许他们到延安采访。同年7月，美国驻延安军事观察组在蒋介石的勉强批准后来到延安，了解八路军的对日作战力量。毛泽东主席、朱德总司令、周恩来副主席、叶剑英总参谋长和彭德怀副总司令等热情地向他们介绍了解放区的情况，请他们到各地参观和到抗日前线访问。为接待美军观察组，中共中央成立了以叶剑英和杨尚昆为正副组长的延安外事组。柯柏年、黄华、陈家康、凌青等为成员，马海德大夫为顾问，担任八路军在美军观察组驻地的联络工作。

抗战胜利后，中国共产党提出实现国内和平的主张。蒋介石在各方压力下同意同中共和谈，并派张治中为代表到延安接毛主席到重庆。美国驻华大使赫尔利同行。

日本投降后，美国大力帮助蒋介石把军队从中国南方运至华北和东北，抢夺抗战果实。1946年初，由张群、周恩来和马歇尔组成的三人委员会决定成立北平军事调处执行部。叶剑英将军为执行部中共方面代表。黄华调北平任执行部中共方面新闻处长。

1946年夏，国民党破坏国共1946年1月10日签署的停战协定，大肆进攻八路军。国共破裂。执行部中共人员于1947年2月撤回延安。

Part Two

Engagement in Party's early foreign affairs activities in Yan'an
(1944 ~ 1947)

Early in the 1940s, Huang Hua was appointed political secretary of Commander-in-Chief Zhu De.

In June 1944, yielding to the strong demand of Chinese and foreign correspondents, the Kuomintang government allowed them to visit Yan'an for news coverage. In July, with Chiang Kai-shek's reluctant approval, a US Military Observer Group (popularly known as the "Dixie Mission") came to Yan'an to investigate the ability of the Eighth Route Army to fight the Japanese. Chairman Mao Zedong, Commander-in-Chief Zhu De, Vice-Chairman Zhou Enlai, Chief of the General Staff Ye Jianying and Deputy Commander-in-Chief Peng Dehuai briefed them on the situation in liberated areas, and invited them to visit various places even the anti-Japanese frontlines. To host the US Military Observer Group, the Central Committee of the CPC set up a Foreign Affairs Group in Yan'an with Ye Jianying and Yang Shangkun as its chief and deputy respectively. Other members, including Ke Bonian, Huang Hua, Chen Jiakang, and Ling Qing, plus Dr. George Hatem as advisor, served at the Americans' quarters as liaison officers with the Eighth Route Army.

After the victory of the anti-Japanese war, the CPC put forward national peace proposals. Chiang Kai-shek under pressure from all sides, agreed to enter into negotiations with the CPC, and sent Zhang Zhizhong as his representative to Yan'an to escort Chairman Mao to Chongqing. US Ambassador to China Patrick Hurley traveled with them.

When Japan surrendered, the US had energetically helped Chiang Kai-shek rush his troops from southern China to northern and northeastern China to seize the fruits of victory of the anti-Japanese war. Early in 1946, a three-man committee composed of Zhang Qun, Zhou Enlai and George Marshall, created the Beiping Military Executive Headquarters. General Ye Jianying was named the CPC representative. Huang Hua became chief of the CPC Information Division of the headquarters.

In the summer of 1946, the Kuomintang tore up the truce agreement concluded on January 10, 1946 between the CPC and the Kuomintang, and launched an all-out offensive against the Eighth Route Army. The negotiations between the two sides broke down. In February 1947, all CPC members in the Headquarters withdrew to Yan'an.

II-1 1944年6月同毛泽东在延安合影。吴印咸摄。
June 1944. Huang Hua with Mao Zedong in Yan'an. *Photo by Wu Yinxian.*

II-2

II-3

II-2 1944年6月，在延安为毛泽东会见《纽约时报》记者阿特金森做翻译。
June 1944. Huang Hua interprets for Mao Zedong being interviewed by Brooks Atkinson of *the New York Times*.

II-3 1944年秋，摄于美军观察组驻地。
Autumn 1944. Huang Hua in the courtyard of the Yenan American Millitary Observer's Group.

Ⅱ-4　1944年6月，接待访问延安的中外记者西北参观团。左三为黄华，左四为马海德。多格·克里弗德医生摄。
June 1944. Huang Hua receives Chinese and foreign correspondents visiting Yan'an. Third left: Huang Hua, fourth left: George Hatem. *Photo by Dr. Doug Clifford.*

Ⅱ-5　陪同美国合众社记者富尔曼参观延安大生产成果展，并向他介绍陕甘宁边区的生产发展情况。
Huang Hua explains to American UP correspondent Harrison Forman development of production in Shaanxi-Gansu-Ningxia Border Region, while accompanying him at Yan'an exhibition.

II-6

II-6 1944年8月7日，同毛泽东和不久前抵延安的美军观察组组长戴维·包瑞德上校在延安飞机场。左一为黄华，时为延安外事组成员。*约翰·高林摄。*

August 7, 1944. Mao Zedong, Col. David Barrett, leader of US Military Observer Group, and Huang Hua (first left) at Yan'an airfield. *Photo by John Colling.*

II-7 1944年7月22日，美军观察组成员的飞机在延安机场着陆后受损。周恩来、杨尚昆立即来至美军驻地慰问驾驶员钱皮恩上尉。左一为谢伟思，右三为黄华。

July 22, 1944. Members of US Military Observer Group .

II-7

II-8

II-8 1944年冬,同朱德总司令、伊顿上校和有吉辛治上士合影。
Winter 1944,together with Commander- in-Chief Zhu De,Colonel Yeaton,and Sergeant Koji Ariyoshi.

II-9

II-9 1944年8月,同延安外事组成员柯柏年、顾问马海德和美军观察组成员多姆克合影。好友马海德(乔治·海德姆)大夫,原籍美国,于1936年经宋庆龄推荐介绍同斯诺一道到达陕北保安。马海德参加了红军,新中国成立后加入了中国国籍。他一生为中国的医疗卫生和对外交往工作作出了出色的贡献。

August 1944. Huang Hua (first right) with members of Foreign Affairs Group in Yan'an (Ke Bonian, George Hatem as advisor) and Domke, a member of US Military Observer Group in Yan'an.Dr. George Hatem (Ma Haide), a good friend, US by origin, in 1936 goes to Bao'an together with Snow on Soong Ching Ling's recommendation. He joins the Red Army. After founding of New China, he becomes a Chinese citizen. He makes outstanding contributions to China's medical and health work as well as foreign contacts all his life.

II-10 1944年9月，第十八集团军副总司令员彭德怀、参谋长叶剑英和军委办公厅主任杨尚昆在延安向包瑞德上校介绍我军前线情况。黄华担任翻译。

September 1944. Peng Dehuai, deputy commander-in-chief of the 18th Group Army, Ye Jianying, chief of staff, and Yang Shangkun, director of General Office of Military Commission, brief Col. Barrett in Yan'an on the situation of the 18th Group Army on the front lines. Huang Hua acts as interpreter.

II-10

II-11

II-11 1944年8月，同美军观察组成员合影。右一为日本血统美籍军官有吉辛治上士，左三为黄华，右二为马海德。
August 1944. Huang Hua with members of US Military Observer Group. First right: Koji Ariyoshi, third left: Huang Hua, second right: George Hatem.

II-12 1944 年 10 月，中方驻美军观察组工作人员合影。左一为谢生，左二为凌青，左四为黄华，右一为柯柏年。
October 1944. Chinese staff members working with US Military Observer Group. First left: Xie Sheng, second left: Ling Qing, fourth left: Huang Hua, first right: Ke Bonian.

II-13 1945 年 3 月,与美军观察组在惠特塞纪念堂前合影。亨利·惠特塞中尉于 1945 年 1 月到太行敌后根据地访问时遭遇日军伏击牺牲。中国翻译李建华同志同时牺牲。朱德为纪念堂题字。前排左三为黄华。
March 1945, in front of Whittlesey Hall together with US Military Observer Group. First Lt. Henry C. Whittlesey was killed by the Japanese snipers during a visit to the Tai Hang anti-Japan base area in Januray 1945, together with Chinese translator Li Jianhua. The names of this memorial hall was written by Commander-in-Chief Zhu De. Third left in the front row:Huang Hua.

II-14 1944年10月，与妻子何理良合影。
October 1944. With wife He Liliang.

II-15 1944年秋，同爱犬阿乌在一起。
Autumn 1944. Huang Hua and his pet dog.

II-16

II-16 1945年8月27日，蒋介石的代表张治中将军(后排左三)和美国驻华大使赫尔利(后排左二)专程到延安陪毛泽东主席同机赴重庆谈判。图为毛泽东接客人至住所途中。左一为参与接待工作的黄华。*约翰·高林摄。*

August 27, 1945. General Zhang Zhizhong (Chiang Kai-shek's representative) and US Ambassador to China Patrick Hurley fly to Yan'an to accompany Chairman Mao Zedong to Chongqing for negotiations. Mao Zedong meets them at Yan'an airfield. First left: Huang Hua, a reception member. *Photo by John Colling.*

II-17

II-17 1946年初，任北平军事调处执行部中共方面新闻处长。图为在执行部总部办公楼（北平协和医院）前留影。
Early 1946. Huang Hua is appointed CPC's chief of Information Division of Military Executive Headquarters. Huang Hua in front of the Headquarters building (Peking Union Medical College).

II-18

II-18　1946年春，北平军事调处执行部中共方面代表叶剑英(前排中)同执行部美方代表罗伯逊(前排左五)和官员们合影。前排左二为李克农，右一为黄华，后排右二为柯柏年，右四为徐冰。

Spring 1946. A group picture of Ye Jianying, CPC representative to the Military Executive Headquarters, with US representative Robertson, and members of the US mission.Center in front row:Ye Jianying,fifth left:Robertson,second left:Li Kenong,first right:Huang Hua,second right in back row:Ke Bonian,fouth right:Xu Bing.

II-19

II-19　1946年春，叶剑英同洛克菲勒基金会官员们合影。前排右一为罗瑞卿，后排自左至右为：柯柏年、苏井观、李克农、黄华。

Spring 1946. Ye Jianying with officials of Rockefeller Foundation. First right in front row: Luo Ruiqing, from left in back row: Ke Bonian, Su Jingguan, Li Kenong, Huang Hua.

II-20

II-20 1946年6月，叶剑英宴请多次向解放区押运宋庆龄创立的中国福利基金募集的医药物资的加拿大籍医生铁尔生·哈里逊。联合国救济总署和解放区救济总署的官员应邀来叶公馆聚会并合影。后排左三为哈里逊，左四为詹姆士·格兰特，前排右一为黄华。1946年冬，哈里逊不顾沿途国民党当局的重重阻挠、严寒和饥饿，把五十多吨物资运抵山东解放区后逝世。

June 1946. Ye Jianying entertains T. Harrison, a Canadian doctor, who has escorted several times to liberated areas convoys of medical supplies, which are raised by China Welfare Fund founded by Soong Ching Ling. Officials of UNRRA (United Nations Relief and Rehabilitation Administration) and CLARA (Chinese Liberated Areas Relief Administration) are also invited to get together at Ye's official residence in Peking. Third left in back row: Dr. Harrison, fourth left: James Grant, first right in front row: Huang Hua. In spite of one obstruction after another by Kuomintang regime throughout his journey as well as severe cold and hunger, Dr. Harrison succeeds in delivering to liberated areas in Shandong the supplies of over 50 tons, but dies afterwards.

第三部分

参与新中国建立初期的外交活动
（1949～1958）

　　1949 年初，人民解放军以排山倒海之势，先后解放了整个东北和华北。4 月强渡长江，南京和上海相继解放。人民军队所到之处，各市军事管制委员会建立之时，外国在中国的特权被一扫而光。以中华人民共和国于 10 月 1 日宣告成立为标志，中华民族获得了真正的独立，中国人民牢牢地掌握了国家的主权。1949 年，黄华先后调天津、南京和上海任军事管制委员会委员和外侨事务处处长，在地方执行新中国的外交政策。

　　新中国在建立之初即在国际舞台上十分活跃。周恩来总理兼外交部长倡导的和平共处五项原则是我国外交政策的指导方针，在国际上得到广泛的共识。

　　1954 年 4 月至 7 月，周恩来率团出席关于和平解决朝鲜问题与恢复印度支那和平问题的日内瓦会议。1955 年 5 月又率团出席亚非团结（万隆）会议。新中国对维护国际和平、反对帝国主义和促进亚非人民团结事业的努力赢得了国际社会的赞誉。

　　黄华参加了这两次会议，担任中国代表团政治顾问和发言人。

Part Three

Participation in diplomatic activities during early years of the founding of New China

(1949 ~ 1958)

Early in 1949, the People's Liberation Army (PLA) liberated the entire Northeast and North China with the momentum of an avalanche. In April, the PLA fought its way across the Yangtze River and liberated Nanjing and Shanghai one after another. With the PLA's entry into the cities, municipal military control commissions were set up. All foreign special privileges in China were swept away. The founding of the People's Republic of China on October 1st marked genuine national independence and firm control of state sovereignty in the hands of the Chinese people. In 1949, Huang Hua was transferred to Tianjin, Nanjing and Shanghai successively as a member of the military control commission and chief of Division of Foreign Nationals' Affairs, implementing New China's foreign policy in those localities.

Since its founding, New China at once played an active role in the international arena. The Five Principles of Peaceful Coexistence initiated by Premier and Foreign Minister Zhou Enlai are the guiding principles of our foreign policy, and have won broad common understanding the world over.

From April to July 1954, Zhou Enlai led a delegation to the Geneva Conference on the Peaceful Settlement of the Korean Question and the Restoration of Peace in Indo-China. In May 1955, he again led another delegation to the Asian-African (Bandung) Conference. New China's efforts for maintaining international peace, opposing imperialism and promoting unity among Asian and African peoples, have been appreciated by the international community.

Huang Hua participated in these two conferences, and was political advisor and spokesman of the Chinese delegation.

III-1 1949年4月，毛泽东在北京香山接见新民主主义青年团代表大会与会者。左一为黄华。

April 1949. Mao Zedong receives in Beijing members attending the Congress of New Democratic Youth League. First left: Huang Hua.

III-2 1949年4月，长期从事党的青年工作和干部培训工作的黄华出席新民主主义青年团第一次全国代表大会，被选为青年团中央委员。前排左二为黄华。

April 1949. Huang Hua (second left in front row) attends the First National Congress of New Democratic Youth League, and is elected member of the Central Committee of the League.

Ⅲ-3 1953年10月26日，黄华以中国人民志愿军代表团政治会议中国政府代表身份同朝鲜政府代表奇石福和美国政府代表迪安在朝鲜板门店开始进行关于和平解决朝鲜问题的政治谈判。正面一排左二为黄华。

October 26, l953. Huang Hua as representative of the Chinese government and the Korean government representative on one side and US representative on the other, take part in political negotiation at Panmunjom for the peaceful settlement of the Korean war question. Second left in front row: Huang Hua.

III-4 1953年10月，与朝鲜
军事停战委员会中国人民志愿军
代表团团长李克农合影。
October 1953. Li Kenong, head
of Chinese People's Volunteers
delegation to the Korean Armi-
stice Commission, with Huang
Hua.

III-5 1953年10月，同参加朝
鲜板门店谈判的中国志愿军代表
团干部在朝鲜开城合影。自左至
右为：田进、朱青、黄华、王楚良、
张启程。
October 1953. Huang Hua and cadres of Chinese People's Volunteers
delegation participating in
Panmunjom talks. From left: Tian
Jin, Zhu Qing, Huang Hua, Wang
Chuliang ,Zhang Qicheng.

Ⅲ-6

Ⅲ-6　1954年4—7月，中华人民共和国总理兼外交部长周恩来出席在瑞士日内瓦举行的和平解决朝鲜问题和恢复印度支那和平问题的国际会议。黄华担任代表团顾问和发言人。图为周恩来同代表团成员在日内瓦花山别墅内边散步边谈工作。右四为张闻天，右二为李克农，左二为王稼祥，右三为黄华。

April to July, 1954. Geneva Conference on Peaceful Settlement of Korean Question and Restoration of Peace in Indo-China, which Chinese Premier and Foreign Minister Zhou Enlai attends. Huang Hua is advisor and spokesman of Chinese delegation. During Geneva Conference in May 1954, Zhou Enlai and members of the Chinese delegation walk and discuss problems at his residence (Villa Montfleury) in Geneva. Fourth right: Zhang Wentian, second right: Li Kenong, second left: Wang Jiaxiang, third right: Huang Hua.

III-7 1954年6月9日，黄华以出席日内瓦会议中国代表团顾问、发言人身份在日内瓦国联大厦举行记者招待会。右二为黄华。

June 9, 1954. Huang Hua (second right) as advisor of Chinese delegation to the Geneva Conference and spokesman of the delegation, holds a press conference at the Palais Des Nations in Geneva.

III-8 1954年6月，接见到日内瓦呼吁恢复印度支那和平的法国巴黎近郊维特里各界代表团。中间者为黄华。

June 1954. Huang Hua (center) receives a people's delegation appealing for restoration of peace in Indo-China from Paris suburbs.

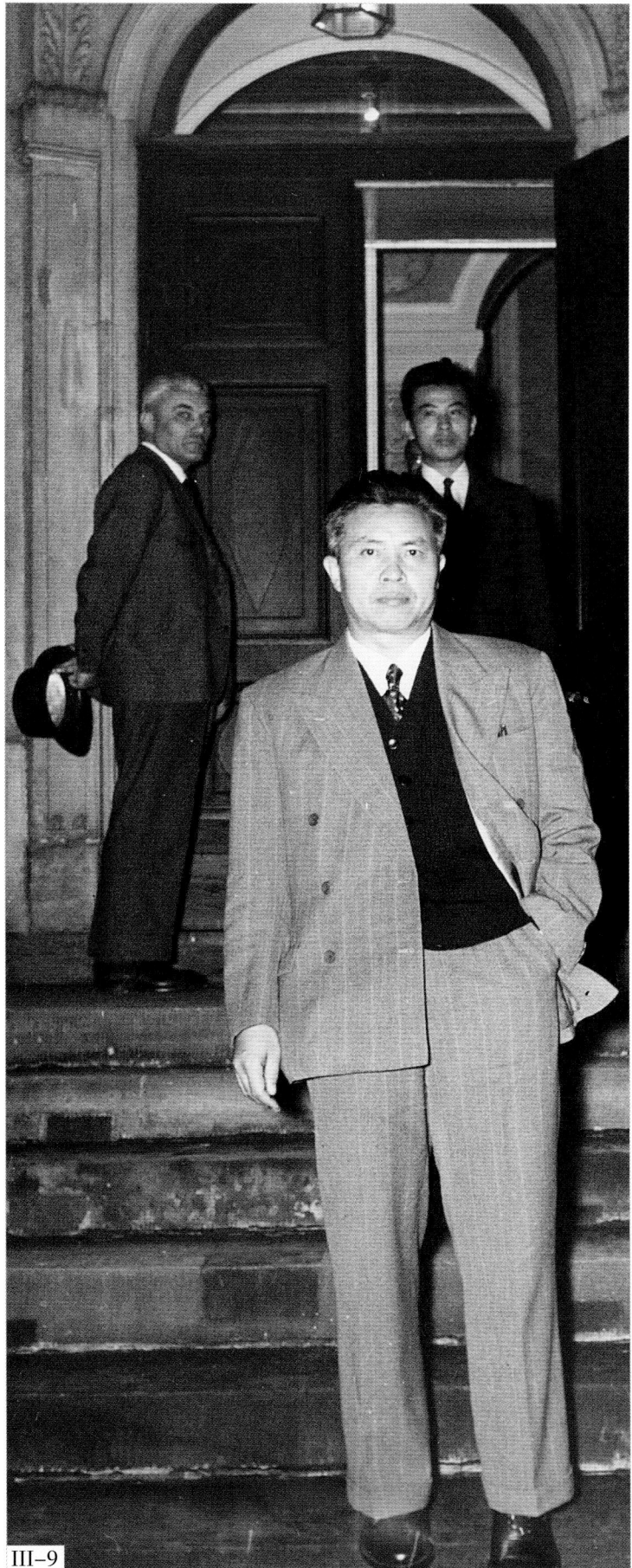

Ⅲ-9　1958年9月15日，中美大使级谈判在波兰复会。图为担任中美大使级谈判顾问的黄华在华沙留影。

September 15, 1958. Sino-US talks at ambassadorial level resume in Poland. Huang Hua in Warsaw as advisor to the talks.

Ⅲ-9

第四部分

出使加纳共和国和阿拉伯联合共和国（埃及）
（1960～1969）

五六十年代,反殖民主义斗争的火焰席卷非洲大陆。殖民地纷纷争得独立，非洲大陆呈现一片朝气蓬勃的景象。中国一贯支持亚、非、拉民族独立运动，同取得独立的国家正式建立外交关系。

1960年黄华任中国首任驻加纳特命全权大使，大力开展工作，广交朋友，促进两国政治、经济关系。恩克鲁玛总统访华和周恩来总理访问加纳更增强了两国的了解、友谊与合作。

1966年至1969年，黄华调任驻阿拉伯联合共和国（埃及）大使。

六十年代，黄华大使曾作为我国政府特使赴坦噶尼喀、毛里求斯和刚果（布）等共和国庆祝独立，同坦噶尼喀和刚果（布）共和国正式建立外交关系。他还访问了加沙地区，出席巴勒斯坦解放组织大会。

Part Four

Appointment to be Ambassador to Republic of Ghana
and United Arab Republic (Egypt)

(1960 ~ 1969)

In the 1950s and 1960s, the flames of anti-colonialist struggle swept across the African continent. One after another, colonial countries strove for independence. The African continent seethed with vigour and vitality. China has all along supported national independence movements in Asia, Africa and Latin America, and established formal diplomatic relations with the countries which have gained independence.

In 1960, Huang Hua was appointed the first Ambassador to Ghana. He devoted major efforts to broaden his work, made friends with people of various circles and promoted bilateral relations in political and economic fields. President Nkrumah's visit to China and Premier Zhou Enlai's visit to Ghana further strengthened the mutual understanding, friendship and cooperation between the two countries.

From 1966 to 1969, Huang Hua was transferred to be Ambassador to the United Arab Republic (Egypt).

In the 1960s, Ambassador Huang Hua as special envoy of the Chinese government visited Tanganyika, Mauritius and Congo (Brazzaville), which celebrated their independence, and helped to bring about China's establishment of diplomatic relations with the Republic of Tanganyika and the Republic of Congo (Brazzaville). He also visited the Gaza Strip and attended a mass meeting of the Palestine Liberation Organization (PLO).

IV-4

IV-4 与加纳总统友好交谈。
Ambassador Huang Hua has a friendly conversation with the Ghanain President.

IV-5 1964年1月12日，周恩来、陈毅不顾月前发生行刺克瓦米·恩克鲁玛总统未遂事件，抵达加纳访问。周恩来、陈毅在总统官邸奥苏城堡与恩克鲁玛总统举行会谈。右一为黄华。

January 12, 1964. Premier Zhou Enlai and Vice-Premier Chen Yi visit Ghana in spite of the attempted assassination of President Nkrumah a month before, and hold talks with the President at his official residence. First right: Huang Hua.

IV-6 1964年1月，周恩来、陈毅在加纳首都阿克拉同驻加纳大使馆全体成员合影。前排右九为黄华。

January 1964. Premier Zhou Enlai and Vice-Premier Chen Yi with the entire staff of the Chinese Embassy in Ghana. Ninth right in front row: Huang Hua.

IV-5

IV-7　1961年12月9日，作为中国政府特使在坦噶尼喀共和国首都达累斯萨拉姆拜会总统朱利叶斯·尼雷尔，祝贺坦国独立。

December 9, 1961. Huang Hua as special envoy of Chinese government, calls on Julius K. Nyerere, President of Tanganyika, in Dar-es-Salaam, to offer congratulations on its independence.

IV-8　拜会坦噶尼喀总统朱利叶斯·尼雷尔，双方代表两国政府达成建立大使级外交关系协议。右一为黄华，中间为胡定一秘书。

Huang Hua and Tanganyikan President Nyerere, on behalf of their respective governments, reach an agreement to establish diplomatic relations between the two countries at ambassadorial level. First right: Huang Hua, center: secretary of the Chinese Embassy in Ghana Hu Dingyi.

IV-9 1962年10月，在加纳首都阿克拉中国驻加纳大使馆宴请美国黑人著名学者Ｗ·Ｅ·Ｂ杜波依斯博士和夫人。右一为黄华。

October 1962. Ambassador Huang Hua entertains Dr. W.E.B. Du Bois, a well-known Afro-American scholar, and Shirley Du Bois at the Chinese Embassy in Accra, Ghana. First right: Huang Hua.

IV-9

IV-10 1964年，古巴社会主义革命统一党领导委员会委员切·格瓦拉访问非洲途经加纳，应邀到中国大使馆做客。自左至右为：黄华、古巴驻加纳大使、切·格瓦拉。

1964. Ernesto Guevara, a Cuban revolutionary leader, while visiting Africa by way of Ghana, is welcomed as a guest at Chinese Embassy. From left: Huang Hua, Cuban Ambassador to Ghana, Ernesto Guevara.

IV-10

IV-11　1966 年 3 月，调任驻阿拉伯联合共和国（埃及）大使。图为 3 月 28 日向贾迈尔·纳塞尔总统递交国书。
March 1966. Huang Hua is appointed Ambassador to the United Arab Republic (Egypt). On March 28, Huang Hua presents his credentials to UAR President Gamal A. Nasser.

IV-12 同驻阿联部分外交使节合影。左一为黄华。
Ambassador Huang Hua (first left) and other diplomatic envoys to the UAR.

IV-12

IV-13

IV-13 1967年5月，出席在加沙地区举行的巴勒斯坦解放组织大会。图为巴解主席赛义德·舒凯里讲话。右二为黄华。
May 1967. Huang Hua attends a mass meeting of the Palestine Liberation Organization (PLO) in Gaza Strip. Ahmed Shukairy, PLO Chairman, delivering a speech. Second right: Huang Hua.

IV-14 1968年3月10日，应邀代表中华人民共和国政府到圣路易斯参加毛里求斯共和国独立庆典。西乌萨加·拉姆古兰总理到机场迎接，双方在机场亲切会谈。

March 10, 1968. Huang Hua as representative of the Chinese government attends independence celebrations of the Republic of Mauritius and has a cordial conversation with Prime Minister Seewoosagur Ramgoolam at Port Louis airport.

IV-15 1968年3月12日，在圣路易斯出席毛里求斯国民议会开幕式。

March 12, 1968. Huang Hua attends the opening ceremony of the National Assembly of Mauritius at Port Louis.

IV-16 黄华在圣路易斯参观华侨书店。黄华右侧为驻埃及大使馆秘书舒暲。Huang Hua visits Overseas Chinese Bookstore at Port Louis. On his right: Shu Zhang, secretary of Chinese Embassy in Egypt.

IV-17 1969年7月黄华大使奉调回国前，五十一位外国驻阿联使节集体赠送刻有每人姓名和国名的纪念银盘。*周幼马摄。* July 1969. Ambassador Huang Hua before being recalled to China , is presented with a silver plate as a souvenir by 51 diplomatic envoys to the UAR engraved with their names and countries. *Photo by Zhou Youma.*

第五部分

在中美关系开始解冻的日子里　出使加拿大

（1970~1971）

　　六十年代，国际形势发生重大变化。中国的国际威望空前提高，美国国内舆论反对越南战争和对华友好的呼声高涨，种种因素促使中美关系走向缓和。

　　1970年8月,中国人民的老朋友埃德加·斯诺及夫人应邀来华到各地访问，黄华全程陪同。10月1日,毛泽东邀斯诺在天安门城楼上一起观看群众游行。12月16日又同斯诺谈话，表示了邀请尼克松总统访华的愿望。

　　1971年7月，美国总统国家安全事务助理基辛格博士应邀秘密来中国访问，叶剑英到机场迎接。周恩来同基辛格会谈。15日双方同时发表公告，标志中美关系开始解冻。

　　1971年7月下旬，黄华奉命调任驻加拿大首任大使。这是中国在北美洲的第一个大使馆。

Part Five

During the days following a thaw in Sino-US relations
Appointment to be Ambassador to Canada

(1970 ~ 1971)

In the 1960s, the international situation underwent major changes. China's international prestige was unprecedentedly enhanced. US public opinion opposing the Vietnam War and befriending China ran high. All these factors impelled a relaxation in Sino-US relations.

In August 1970, Edgar Snow, an old friend of the Chinese people, and his wife were invited to China and accompanied by Huang Hua throughout the trip. On October 1st, Mao Zedong asked Snow to watch the mass parade together with him on the Tian'anmen rostrum. On December 16, Mao Zedong again had a talk with Snow, and expressed his desire to invite President Nixon to visit China.

In July 1971, Dr. Henry Kissinger, National Security Assistant to US President, was invited to visit China in secret, and Ye Jianying went to the airport to welcome him. Zhou Enlai held talks with Dr. Kissinger. On July 15, the two sides issued a joint announcement which marked the beginning of a thaw in Sino-US relations.

In the later part of July 1971, Huang Hua, as China's first Ambassador to Canada, opens China's first embassy in North America.

V-1

V-1 1970年8月，美国友好人士埃德加·斯诺及夫人应邀访问中国，受到毛泽东接见。图为黄华陪同周恩来在北京首都体育馆亲切会见斯诺及夫人。右二为黄华。
August 1970. Premier Zhou Enlai accompanied by Huang Hua, has a cordial meeting with Snow and Mrs. Snow in Beijing. Second right: Huang Hua.

V-2 34年后，黄华陪伴埃德加·斯诺重访保安，在毛泽东旧居前留影。
Edgar Snow accompanied by Huang Hua revisits Bao'an after 34 years. In front of former residence of Mao Zedong.

V-2

V-3 1971年7月9日，美国总统国家安全事务助理基辛格应邀秘密访华抵京，叶剑英到南苑军用机场欢迎。左起为冀朝铸、叶剑英、熊向晖、黄华、基辛格、章文晋、唐闻生。

July 9, 1971. Ye Jianying welcomes Dr. Kissinger, National Security Assistant to US President, on a secret visit to China. Also present, from left: Ji Chaozhu, Ye Jianying, Xiong Xianghui, Huang Hua, Kissinger, Zhang Wenjin, Tang Wensheng.

V-4

V-4　1971年7月，周恩来同基辛格会谈数次后，双方决定于7月15日同时发表中美会谈公告，宣布美国总统尼克松应中国政府邀请即将访华。《公告》在国际上产生巨大的震动。图为叶剑英同基辛格在钓鱼台国宾馆五号楼会晤。左一为黄华。

July 1971. After several talks between Premier Zhou Enlai and Dr.Kissinger, both sides issue an announcement on July 15 on the forthcoming visit to China by US President Nixon at the invitation of Chinese government, which startles the world. Ye Jianying meets with Dr. Kissinger at Diaoyutai State Guest House. First left: Huang Hua.

V-5

V-5　1971年7月23日，作为中国首任驻加拿大大使抵达渥太华，在机场受到加拿大政府官员的热烈欢迎。图为热情的欢迎群众挥舞中加两国国旗迎接黄华大使。

July 23, 1971. Huang Hua, as China's first Ambassador to Canada, is warmly welcomed by Canadian officials on his arrival in Ottawa. Cheering people wave Chinese and Canadian flags to welcome Ambassador Huang Hua.

V-6　1971年7月27日，向加拿大副总督威尔弗莱德·贾德森递交国书。
July 27, 1971. Ambassador Huang Hua presents his credentials to Canadian Deputy Governor-General, Wilfred Judson.

V-7 1971年8月13日，拜会加拿大总理皮埃尔·特鲁多。加拿大新闻社彼得·普瑞格摄。
August 13, 1971. Ambassador Huang Hua calls on Canadian Prime Minister Pierre Trudeau. *Photo by Peter Pregg, Canadian Press*.

第六部分

出任常驻联合国和安理会代表
（ 1971 ～ 1976 ）

六十年代，世界的潮流进一步向着有利于人民的方向发展，国际社会反对孤立中国的呼声日益高涨。1971 年 10 月 25 日，第二十六届联合国大会以压倒多数票通过 2758 号决议，恢复中华人民共和国在联合国的席位及其所属一切组织的代表权。这是世界上广大中小国家尤其是亚非拉国家长期斗争的结果，是国际正义的胜利。自此，中国全面展开多边外交。

中国在联合国组织的各种活动中坚决支持第三世界的合理主张，团结广大中小国家，反对帝国主义、殖民主义和强权政治，为维护联合国的宗旨和原则，建立公正的国际政治经济秩序而斗争。在第六届特别联大上，邓小平副总理庄严宣布，中国永远属于第三世界，永远不称霸，受到广大中小国家的欢迎。

Part Six

Appointment to be Permanent Representative to the United Nations and its Security Council
(1971~1976)

In the 1960s, world trends further developed in a direction favorable to the people, and the voice of the international community opposing the isolation of China rose day by day. On October 25, 1971, the 26th UN General Assembly passed Resolution 2758 by an overwhelming majority, restoring the seat of the People's Republic of China in the United Nations and China's representation in all its affiliated organizations. This was the result of protracted struggle waged by numerous small and medium-sized countries, especially Asian, African and Latin American countries, and was a victory for international justice. From then on, China has carried out its multilateral diplomacy in an all-round way.

In its UN activities, China has resolutely supported rational proposals of the Third World, stood on the side of small and medium-sized countries, opposed imperialism, colonialism and power politics, and has striven to safeguard the purposes and principles of the United Nations in building a just, political and economic world order. Vice-Premier Deng Xiaoping at the Sixth Special Session of UN General Assembly solemnly declared that China will always belong to the Third World and will never seek hegemony. A great many small and medium-sized countries have welcomed China's pledge.

VI-1　1971年11月14日，出席联合国第二十六届大会的中国代表团正、副团长乔冠华和黄华拜会生病住院的联合国秘书长吴丹，并递交了全权证书。右一为黄华。*联合国永田摄。*

November 14, 1971. Qiao Guanhua, head, and Huang Hua, deputy head, of the Chinese delegation to the 26th UN General Assembly, call on hospitalized UN Secretary — General U Thant and present their documents of full powers. First right: Huang Hua. *Photo by Nagata of UN.*

VI-2 1971年11月15日，中国出席联合国第二十六届大会代表团在大会厅就座。前排左起：乔冠华、黄华、符浩。后排左起：唐闻生、熊向晖、陈楚。

November 15, 1971. Members of the Chinese delegation attending the 26th UN General Assembly. From left in front row: Qiao Guanhua, Huang Hua, Fu Hao. From left in back row: Tang Wensheng, Xiong Xianghui, Chen Chu.

VI–3 1971 年 12 月 4 日，作为中国常驻联合国和安全理事会代表出席安理会会议。图为黄华在讲话。*联合国 T·陈摄。*
December 4, 1971. Huang Hua as China's Permanent Representative to UN and its Security Council, attends a Security Council session. Huang Hua speaking at the session. *Photo by T. Chen of UN.*

VI–4 同一些国家的常驻联合国代表合影。右二为黄华。

Huang Hua and some permanent representatives of other countries to the UN. Second right: Huang Hua.

VI–5 同非殖民化委员会主席萨里姆大使（坦桑尼亚）交谈。

Huang Hua chats with Ambassador S.A. Salim (Tanzania), Chairman of the Decolonization Commission.

VI-6　1972年2月14日，同墨西哥大使罗布洛斯互祝中墨两国谈判建交达成协议。

February 14, 1972. Huang Hua and Mexican Ambassador Alfonso Garcia Robles congratulate each other on reaching an agreement to establish diplomatic relations between the two countries.

VI-6

VI-7

VI-7　1972年2月，出席安全理事会审议葡属殖民地问题的亚的斯亚贝巴会议。

February 1972. Huang Hua attends Addis Abeba session of the UN Security Council in discussion of the issue of Portuguese colonies.

HUANG HUA

VI–8　1972 年 2 月，在亚的斯亚贝巴拜会埃塞俄比亚皇帝海尔·塞拉西。左一为俞沛文大使。
February 1972. Huang Hua calls on His Imperial Majesty Emperor Haile Selassie of Ethiopia, in Addis Abeba.
First left: Ambassador Yu Peiwen.

VI-9

VI-9 1973年3月，中国代表团自纽约飞抵巴拿马市出席审议巴拿马运河问题的安全理事会会议。巴拿马共和国旅游部部长陪同。会议厅外广场上的右侧标语写着巴拿马政府首脑奥玛尔·托里霍斯义愤填膺的话："有哪个国家能忍受耻辱让别国的国旗插在她的心脏上？！"巴拿马运河区地处巴拿马的中央，属美国政府管辖。这种状态侵犯巴拿马国家主权，极度伤害巴拿马人民的民族感情。

March 1973. Chinese delegation, arriving in Panama from New York, attends a session of the UN Security Council in discussion of the issue of the Panama Canal, accompanied by Panamanian Minister of Tourism. Outside the conference hall, a slogan in the words of Omar Torrijos, head of the Panamanian government, filled with indignation: "What nation of the world can withstand the humiliation of a foreign flag piercing its own heart?!" The Panama Canal is located in the center of Panama, but under US jurisdiction. Such situation extremely violates Panama's sovereignty and hurts national feelings of the Panamanian people.

VI-10　1974年4月10日，出席联合国大会第六届特别会议的中国代表团团长邓小平在联合国大会第六届特别会议发言后，各国代表前来祝贺。正面左一为黄华。

April 10, 1974. Deng Xiaoping, head of the Chinese delegation attending the 6th Special Session of the UN General Assembly, is congratulated by representatives of various countries after his speech at the session. First left in front: Huang Hua.

VI-11　1975年9月，与联合国大会第七届特别会议主席布特弗利卡合影。

September 1975. Huang Hua and Abdelaziz Bouteflika, Chairman of the 7th Special Session of UN General Assembly.

VI-12　1974年9月23日，联合国五个常任理事国代表同联合国秘书长合影。左起：黄华、希拉克、基辛格、瓦尔德海姆、葛罗米柯、卡拉汉。*联合国T·陈摄。*

September 23, 1974. Five representatives of permanent members of the UN Security Council with UN Secretary-General Kurt Waldheim. From left: Huang Hua, Jacques Chirac, Kissinger, Waldheim, Andrei A. Gromyko, James Callaghan. *Photo by T. Chen of UN.*

VI-13 同联合国海洋法会议主席汉密尔顿·阿梅拉辛格（斯里兰卡）合影。
Huang Hua and Hamilton Amerasinghe (Sri Lanka), Chairman of the UN Conference on the Law of the Sea.

VI–14

VI–14 1976年9月10日，联合国安全理事会为毛泽东主席逝世默哀。*联合国索·路因摄。*
September 10, 1976. UN Security Council members stand in silent tribute to Chairman Mao Zedong who has just passed away.
Photo by Saw Lwin of UN.

VI-15 1982年9月，同中国常驻联合国代表凌青大使合影。
September 1982. Foreign Minister Huang Hua and Ambassador Ling Qing, Chinese Permanent Representative to the UN.

VI-16 1992年6月11日，同联合国副秘书长谢启美在纽约合影。
June 11, 1992. Huang Hua and UN Under-Secretary-General Xie Qimei in New York.

VI-17 1982年,同联合国人口活动基金执行主任纳菲斯·萨迪克博士合影。
1982. Foreign Minister Huang Hua and Dr. Nafis Sadik, Executive Director of the UN Fund for Population Activities.

VI-18 1981年6月,在北京同联合国副秘书长布莱德福·摩尔斯会面。
June 1981. Huang Hua meets with Bradford Morse, Under-Secretary-General of the UN .

第七部分

主持外交部工作

（1976～1982）

1976年12月，黄华被任命为外交部长时，正值文化大革命结束，百废待举。邓小平主持中央工作，大力拨乱反正，提出改革开放的总方针。他以战略家的眼光对外交方针政策提出了一系列英明独到的创见和指示，使我国的外交工作出现了大好局面和新的突破。在这个时期，签订了对中日两国和人民有极重要意义的《中日和平友好条约》。邓小平副总理访问日本，出席两国批准书的互换仪式，以示重视。中国同美国正式建立外交关系，在国际政治生活中产生了重大影响。建交谈判时遗留的美国售台武器问题，通过艰苦谈判于1982年8月17日达成协议。在邓小平一国两制的构想指导下，中英两国政府开始对香港回归祖国问题进行谈判。这个时期，中国和印度、苏联的关系有所改善。

在毛泽东和周恩来的领导和培育下，外交部建立了一支素质良好和业务熟练的干部队伍。外交工作的成绩是中央的英明决策和外交部门团队的敬业精神结合的成果。

Part Seven

Taking Charge of the Ministry of Foreign Affairs

(1976～1982)

In December 1976, Huang Hua was appointed Minister of Foreign Affairs. As the Cultural Revolution had just ended, many neglected tasks remained to be done. Being in charge of the work of the Central Committee of the Communist Party of China, Deng Xiaoping arduously brought order out of chaos, and put forward a policy of reform and opening-up. With the foresight of a strategist, he advanced a series of brilliant original ideas and instructions of foreign policy, making China's diplomacy achieve a good situation and new breakthrough. During this period, the Treaty of Peace and Friendship Between China and Japan was signed, which was of great significance to the peoples of both countries. In order to attach importance to it, Vice-Premier Deng Xiaoping visited Japan and attended the ceremony for exchanging the instruments of ratification of the Treaty. China and the United States established formal diplomatic relations, producing a great impact on international political life. On the issue of arms sale to Taiwan by the United States which had been left over during negotiations for diplomatic relations, an agreement was reached after tough negotiations on August 17, l982. Under the guidance of Deng Xiaoping's concept of "one country and two systems", China and U.K. started negotiations for the return of Hong Kong to the motherland. In this period, relations between China and India, and between China and the Soviet Union were also improved to some extent.

Under the leadership and nurture of Mao Zedong and Zhou Enlai, the Ministry of Foreign Affairs trained a contingent of cadres, who were of good quality and proficient in work. The achievements obtained in the field of foreign affairs were attributable to the wise decisions of the Party and the team spirit and dedication to work of the cadres in various departments of foreign affairs.

VII-1

VII-1 1977年9月29日，黄华外长在联合国第三十二届大会全体会议上发言。
September 29, 1977. Foreign Minister Huang Hua delivers a speech at the plenary session of the 32nd UN General Assembly.

VII-2 1978年9月8日，陪同赴平壤参加朝鲜民主主义人民共和国成立三十周年庆祝活动的中国党政代表团团长邓小平在平壤锦绣山议事堂拜会金日成主席并赠送礼品。后排右一为黄华。

September 8,1978. Accompanied by Huang Hua, Deng Xiaoping leads a delegation of the Chinese Communist Party and Government to attend the celebration of 30th Anniversary of the founding of DPR of Korea presenting a gift to President Kim Il Sung. First right in back row: Huang Hua.

VII–3　1978年6月，拜会土耳其总统法赫里·科鲁蒂尔克。
June 1978. Huang Hua calls on Fahri Koruturk, President of Turkey.

VII–4　1978年9月，同希腊外长乔治·拉利斯在雅典签署中希文化协议。后排左一为西欧司司长宋之光。
September 1978. Huang Hua and George Rallis, Foreign Minister of Greece, sign an agreement of cultural cooperation between the two countries in Athens. First left in back row: Song Zhiguang, Director of Western European Affairs Department of Foreign Ministry.

VII-5

VII-5 1978年10月5日，应邀访问意大利。图为10月8日在罗马拜访阿力山德罗·佩尔蒂尼总统。
October 8,1978. During his visit to Italy, Huang Hua calls on Italian President Alessandro Pertini in Rome.

VII-6 1978年10月，在伦敦唐宁街10号拜访英国首相詹姆士·卡拉汉。
October 1978. Huang Hua calls on James Callaghan, British Prime Minister, at 10 Downing Street, London.

VII-6

VII-7

VII-7 1978年8月12日，《中日和平友好条约》签字仪式在北京人民大会堂举行。图为中国外交部长黄华和日本外相园田直分别代表本国政府在条约上签字后互换文本。

August 12,1978. The Treaty of Peace and Friendship Between China and Japan is signed in Beijing. Huang Hua and Sunao Sonoda, Foreign Ministers of both countries, sign the Treaty and exchange texts.

VII-8

邓小平副総理　黄華外交部長　園田外務大臣　福田総理大

VII-8　1978年10月23日，在东京首相府内举行的中日两国议会对《中日和平友好条约》批准书的互换仪式上。自左至右为：邓小平、黄华、园田直、福田赳夫。

October 23, 1978. At a ceremony in Tokyo for exchanging the instruments of ratification of the Treaty by the legislatures of both countries. From left: Deng Xiaoping, Huang Hua, Sunao Sonoda, Takeo Fukuda.

VII-9

VII-9 1978年10月24日，邓小平一行到住宅看望1972年决定同中国恢复邦交的日本前首相田中角荣。左二为黄华。

October 24, 1978. Deng Xiaoping visits Kakuei Tanaka, former Prime Minister of Japan, at his residence. Tanaka decided to establish diplomatic relations with China in 1972. Second left: Huang Hua.

VII-10

VII-10 邓小平、福田赳夫、园田直、黄华签名的纪念《中日和平友好条约》生效的首日封。邮戳日期为1978年10月22日。

A commemorative postcard, stamped with a postmark of October 22, 1978, for the day of the Treaty taking effect, autographed by Deng Xiaoping, Takeo Fukuda, Sunao Sonoda and Huang Hua.

VII–11 1978年11月5日，陪同邓小平访问泰国。邓小平在同泰国总理江萨·差玛南举行会谈前亲切握手。右三为黄华。
November 5,1978. Accompanied by Huang Hua, Deng Xiaoping visits Thailand and before talks, shakes hands with Gen. Kriangsak Chamanan, Prime Minister of Thailand. Third right: Huang Hua.

VII–12 同泰国外长乌巴蒂·巴乍里央恭互换中泰贸易和科技合作协议签字书。
Exchange of texts of the signed agreement of trade, scientific and technological cooperation by Huang Hua and Upadit Pachariyangkul, Foreign Minister of Thailand.

VII-13

VII-13 1978 年 11 月 12 日，陪同邓小平和新加坡总理李光耀在新加坡总理府举行会谈。左二为黄华。
November 12,1978. Accompanied by Huang Hua, Deng Xiaoping holds talks with Lee Kuan Yew, Prime Minister of Singapore,
in Lee's office. Second left: Huang Hua.

VII-14　1979年1月29日,参加邓小平与卡特在白宫举行的会谈。
January 29, 1979. Accompanied by Huang Hua, Deng Xiaoping holds talks with President Jimmy Carter at the White House.

VII-15　中美两国通过谈判决定建立正式外交关系。1978年12月16日两国政府同时发表联合公报。图为《人民日报》首页。
December 16, 1978. A joint communique issued simultaneously by China and the United States on establishment of formal diplomatic relations. *The People's Daily* carries the news.

VII-16 1979年1月30日，出席在华盛顿中国驻美国大使馆举行的庆祝中美建交招待会。在招待会上，中国人民的老朋友海伦·斯诺将毛泽东于1937年介绍她去山西太行山根据地写给邓小平的信于四十二年后亲自交给邓小平。左一为杨洁篪，左三为韩叙大使，右二为黄华夫人何理良。 康西丁摄。

January 30,1979. At a reception held in the Chinese Embassy in Washington, Helen Snow, an old friend of the Chinese people, hands over a letter to Deng Xiaoping to whom the letter was written by Chairman Mao in 1937, introducing Helen Snow to visit base area in Taihang Mountains of Shanxi. First left:Yang Jiechi,third left: Ambassador Han Xu,second right: He Liliang. *Photo by Tim Considine*.

VII-17 同美国民主党参议员曼斯菲尔德友好叙谈。

A friendly chat with American Democratic Senator Mike Mansfield.

VII–18 1979 年 9 月 18 日，陪同美国前总统理查德·尼克松在北京参观。
September 18,1979. Accompanied by Huang Hua, former US President Richard Nixon visits Beijing.

VII–19 1979 年 10 月 16 日，应邀访问法国期间，拜会吉斯卡尔·德斯坦总统。
October 16, 1979. During his visit to France, Huang Hua calls on President Giscard d'Estaing.

VII-20 1979年11月4日，应邀访问圣马力诺共和国，检阅仪仗队。这是中国外长第一次访问圣马力诺。
November 4, 1979. Huang Hua reviews a guard of honor during his visit to San Marino, the first ever official visit by a Chinese Foreign Minister.

VII-21 同圣马力诺外交和政务部长焦尔达诺·布鲁诺·雷菲会谈。
Huang Hua holds talks with Giordano Bruno Reffi, Minister of Foreign and Political Affairs of San Marino.

VII-22　1979年11月8日，访问南斯拉夫。图为在布里俄尼拜访南斯拉夫社会主义联邦共和国总统布·约·铁托。
November 8,1979. During his visit to Yugoslavia, Huang Hua calls on President Tito.

VII-23

VII-23　1979年11月20日，应邀访问尼泊尔。图为拜会尼泊尔国王比兰德拉。
November 20,1979. During his visit to Nepal, Huang Hua calls on his Majesty King Birendra.

VII-24　1979年11月20日，在加德满都同尼泊尔王国外交大臣沙希签署边界联合检查议定书。
November 20,1979. Huang Hua and K.B.Shahi, Minister of Foreign Affairs of Nepal, sign in Kathmandu the Protocal on Joint Border Inspection.

VII-24

VII–25　1979 年 12 月，应中国政府邀请，日本首相大平正芳访华。图为 12 月 6 日邓小平在北京人民大会堂同大平正芳一行举行会谈。黄华参加了会谈。

December 6, 1979. Deng Xiaoping holds talks with visiting Japanese Prime Minister Masayoshi Ohira in the Great Hall of the People. Huang Hua participating in the talks.

VII–26　12 月 9 日，陪同大平正芳及夫人志华子访问西安，并将大平首相在陕西省博物馆书写的墨宝"温古知新"复印六十份赠送日本朋友。前排右一为大平志华子，右二为黄华。

照片由大平裕提供。

December 9. Accompanied by Huang Hua, Prime Minister Masayoshi Ohira and Mme. Shigeko Ohira visit Xi'an. Huang Hua distributes 60 copies among Japanese friends of M. Ohira's calligraphy "Understand the present by reviewing the past". First right in front row: Shigeko Ohira, second right: Huang Hua. *Photo provided by Yukata Ohira.*

VII–27　1980 年 1 月 19 日，应邀访问巴基斯坦，同外交部长阿迦·夏希在伊斯兰堡外交部会谈。右排中间为黄华，黄华左侧为徐以新大使。

January 19,1980. During his visit to Pakistan, Huang Hua holds talks with Pakistani Foreign Minister Agha Shaghi in Islamabad. Center in right row: Huang Hua, on his left: Ambassador Xu Yixin.

VII–28　出席巴基斯坦外长阿迦·夏希举行的招待会。右二为黄华。左二为徐以新大使。

Huang Hua attends a reception given by Pakistani Foreign Minister Agha Shaghi. Second right: Huang Hua. Second left: Ambassador Xu Yixin.

VII-29 1980年3月11日，应邀访问菲律宾。菲律宾外长罗慕洛到马尼拉机场欢迎。

March 11,1980. Huang Hua visits the Philippines. Foreign Minister Carlos Romulo welcomes him at the Manila airport.

VII-30 1980年3月12日，同菲律宾外长罗慕洛会谈。

March 12,1980. Huang Hua holds talks with Foreign Minister Romulo.

VII-31　1980 年 4 月 19 日，作为中国政府特使参加津巴布韦共和国独立庆典后，在索尔兹伯里总理府拜会津巴布韦总理穆加贝。April 19,1980. As special envoy of Chinese government, Huang Hua visits Zimbabwe for the celebration of its independence and calls on Prime Minister Mugabe of Zimbabwe in Salisbury.

VII-32　1980 年 4 月 20 日，应邀访问莫桑比克。图为在马普托莫桑比克总统府拜会萨莫拉总统。April 20,1980. During his visit to Mozambique, Huang Hua calls on President Samora Machel in Maputo.

VII-33　1980年6月10日，在斯德哥尔摩皇宫拜会瑞典国王卡尔十六世·古斯塔夫。
June 10, 1980. Huang Hua calls on Swedish King Karl XVI Gustaf at the Palace in Stockholm.

VII-34　1982年6月，应邀访问西班牙，同外交大臣费利佩·德拉莫雷纳会见。
June 1982. During his visit to Spain, Huang Hua meets with the foreign minister of Spain Mr.Felipe de la Morena.

VII-35 1980年6月12日，访问挪威王国。图为会见挪威外交大臣弗里登伦。
June 12, 1980. Huang Hua visits Norway and meets with Foreign Minister Frydenlund.

VII-36 1980年6月19日，应邀访问联邦德国。图为6月20日在波恩拜会总理赫尔穆特·施密特。左一为张彤大使。
June 19,1980. During his visit to Germany, Huang Hua calls on Chancellor Helmudt Schmidt in Bonn. First left: Ambassador Zhang Tong.

VII-37

VII-37　1980年8月16日，和夫人何理良陪同西哈努克亲王和夫人莫尼克公主游览密云水库。

August 16,1980. Accompanied by Huang Hua and He Liliang, Prince Norodom Sihanouk and Princess Monique visit Miyun Reservoir.

VII-38　1980年9月2日，在北京机场迎接前来访问的日本外相伊东正义。
September 2, 1980. At the Beijing airport, Huang Hua welcomes Japanese Foreign Minister Masayoshi Ito.

VII-39　同日本外相伊东正义会谈。伊东正义表示：日本政府要落实大平正芳首相的诺言，向中国提供大额低息长期贷款。左四为黄华。
Huang Hua holds talks with Japanese Foreign Minister Masayoshi Ito who affirms that the Japanese government will carry out the promise made by Prime Minister Masayoshi Ohira to provide ODA to China. Fourth left: Huang Hua.

VII-40 1980年9月30日，应邀在斯特拉斯堡欧洲委员会议会上发表关于中国外交政策的讲话。

September 30, 1980. Huang Hua delivers a speech on China's foreign policy at the Parliamentary Assembly of the Council of Europe in Strasbourg.

VII-41 欧洲委员会为纪念黄华副总理兼外交部长向该委员会讲演而发行的纪念封。

A commemorative envelope issued by the Council of Europe to mark Vice-Premier and Foreign Minister Huang Hua's speech.

VII-42

VII-42　1980年10月2日，应邀访问英国期间，在伦敦唐宁街10号英国首相府拜会英国首相玛格丽特·撒切尔夫人。

October 2,1980. During his visit to Britain, Huang Hua calls on British Prime Minister Margaret Thatcher at 10 Downing Street, London.

VII–43　1981年6月26日，应邀访问印度。图为在会谈前同纳拉辛哈·拉奥外长在外交部留影。右一为申健大使，右二为黄华。《印度时报》记者摄。

June 26, 1981. During his visit to India, Huang Hua is photographed with Indian Foreign Minister Narasimha Rao at Indian Foreign Ministry before talks. First right: Ambassador Shen Jian, second right: Huang Hua. *Photo by a correspondent of the "Times of India".*

VII–44　印中友协成员到机场热情欢迎黄华。

Members of the India-China Friendship Association warmly welcome Huang Hua at the airport.

VII-45　1981年6月28日，拜会印度总理英迪拉·甘地夫人。左一为黄华，右一为何理良。
June 28,1981. Huang Hua calls on Indian Prime Minister Indira Gandhi. First left: Huang Hua, first right: He Liliang.

VII-46 1981年6月28日，同印度人民院议员、印度总理的长子拉杰夫·甘地合影。

June 28,1981. With Rajiv Gandhi, a parliamentarian of the People's House of India and elder son of Indian Prime Minister.

VII-47 1981年6月29日，在中国驻印度大使馆同全印柯棣华大夫纪念委员会主席B·K·巴苏大夫合影。巴苏大夫和其他四位医生于中国抗日战争初年由印度国大党派遣来华任抗日前线战地医生。右四为巴苏，左三为黄华。

June 29, 1981. At the Chinese Embassy in New Delhi. Fourth right: Dr. B.K. Basu, Chairman of the All India Kotnis Memorial Committee. He and four other medical doctors were sent to China by the Indian National Congress Party to serve as frontline doctors in 1938 after outbreak of the war of resistance against Japan. Third left: Huang Hua.

VII-48

VII-48　1981年6月30日，应邀访问斯里兰卡。图为拜会总统朱尼厄斯·理查德·贾亚瓦德纳。右一为斯里兰卡外长阿卜杜勒·卡德尔·萨胡尔·哈米德。

June 30,1981. During his visit to Sri Lanka, Huang Hua calls on President Junius Richard Jayewardene of Sri Lanka. First right: Foreign Minister Abdul Hameed of Sri Lanka.

VII-49 1981年7月3日，应邀访问马尔代夫，同外长法图拉·贾米勒友好会谈。图为在马累出席招待会的情况。

July 3,1981. Huang Hua holds friendly talks with Maldive's Foreign Minister Fathulla Jameel and attends a reception held in Male.

VII-50

VII-50　1981年8月1日，在墨西哥坎昆城出席关于合作与发展的国际会议外长级预备会议。圆桌左边穿浅色衣服者为黄华。

August 1,1981. Huang Hua attends foreign ministers' preparatory meeting of the Conference of Cooperation and Development in Cancun, Mexico. On the left wearing a light-colored suit: Huang Hua.

VII-51 1981年8月1日，在墨西哥坎昆会议上同联邦德国、沙特阿拉伯、印度等国外长叙谈。右二为黄华。

August 1,1981. Huang Hua chats with foreign ministers of Germany, Saudi Arabia and India in Cancun. Second right: Huang Hua.

VII-52 1981年8月2日，在坎昆会议期间同美国国务卿亚历山大·黑格讨论美售台武器问题，争论激烈。双方商定在近期内在华盛顿继续讨论这一问题。

August 2, 1981. In Cancun, Huang Hua discusses U.S. arms sale to Taiwan with Alexander Haig, U.S. Secretary of State. After heated dispute, they decide to continue their talks in Washington in the near future.

VII-53

VII-53 1981 年 10 月 29 日，在华盛顿同美国总统里根、副总统布什、国务卿黑格会谈。
October 29,1981. Vice-Premier and Foreign Minister Huang Hua holds talks with President Reagan, Vice President Bush and Secretary of State Haig in Washington D.C.

VII–54　1981年8月3日，应邀访问委内瑞拉。8月5日拜会委内瑞拉总统埃路易斯·雷拉·坎平斯。
August 5,1981. During his visit to Venezuela, Huang Hua calls on President Luis Herrera Campins.

VII–55

VII–55 1981年8月8日，在波哥大总统府拜会哥伦比亚总统图尔瓦伊·阿亚拉。

August 8,1981. Huang Hua calls on Colombian President Julio Turbay Ayala in Bogota.

VII–56 1981年8月7日，应邀访问哥伦比亚。在波哥大机场受到哥伦比亚外长卡洛斯·莱莫斯的欢迎。

August 7,1981. Huang Hua is welcomed by Colombian Foreign Minister Carlos Lemos at Bogota airport.

VII–56

VII-57 1981 年 9 月 9 日，陪同邓小平在北京人民大会堂会见来访的埃及副总理兼外长卡迈勒·哈桑·阿里。
September 9,1981. Accompanied by Huang Hua, Deng Xiaoping meets with visiting Egyptian Deputy Prime Minister and Foreign Minister Kamal Hassan Aly at the Great Hall of the People.

VII-58 1981 年 10 月 8 日，同来访的巴勒斯坦解放组织主席阿拉法特会谈。左三为黄华。
October 8, 1981. Huang Hua holds talks with PLO Chairman Yasser Arafat in Beijing. Third left: Huang Hua.

VII-59 1981年11月
16日，应邀访问尼日利
亚。尼日利亚副总统亚
历克斯·埃奎梅到拉各
斯机场迎接。
November 16, 1981.
Huang Hua is welcomed
by Vice President Alex
Ekwueme at Lagos airport
when he visits Nigeria.

VII-60 在拉各斯总
统府拜会尼日利亚总统
谢胡乌斯曼·阿里尤·沙
加里。
Huang Hua calls on Nige-
rian President Shehu
Usman Aliyu Shagari in
Lagos.

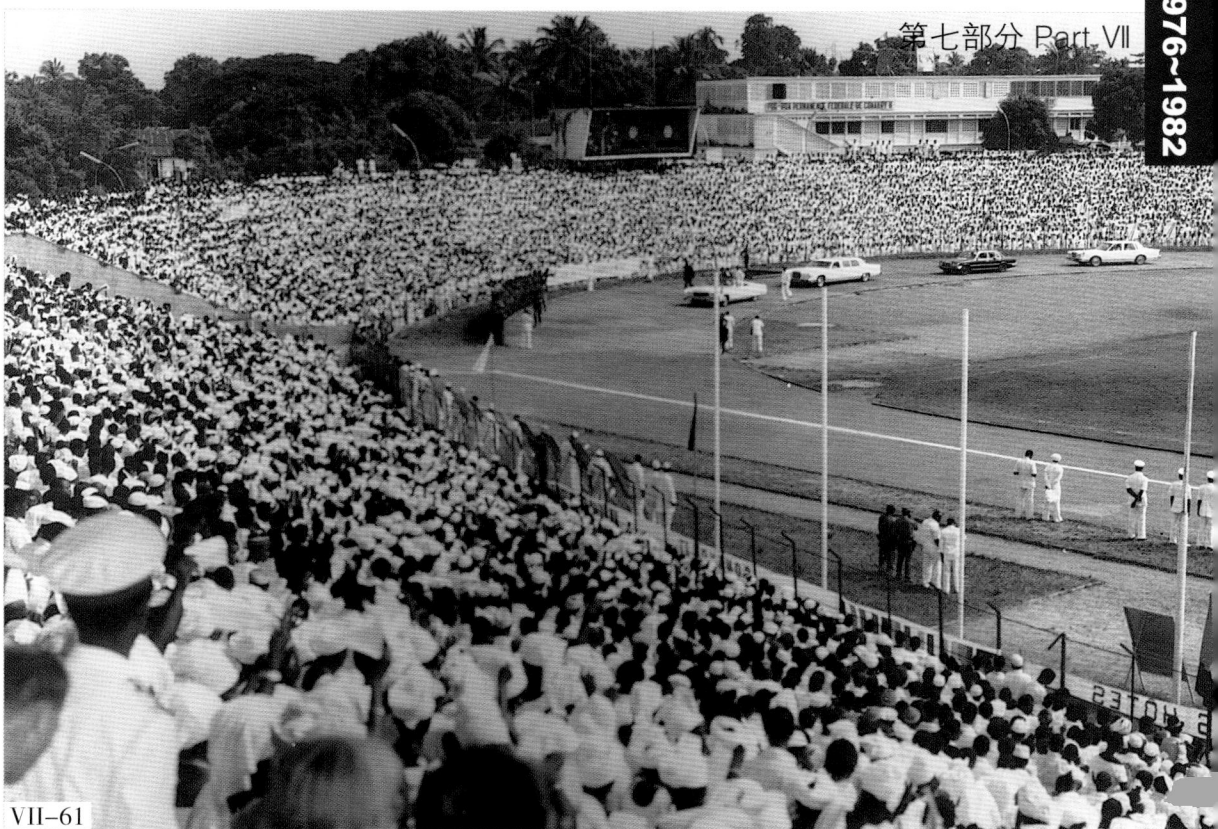

VII-61 1981年11月20日，应邀访问几内亚。在科纳克里同塞古·杜尔总统乘敞篷汽车向几内亚首都人民致意。

November 20, 1981. Huang Hua visits Republic of Guinea, saluting local people with President Sekou Toure in an open car in Conakry.

VII-61

VII-62

VII-62 1981年11月22日，几内亚总统塞古·杜尔在科纳克里向应邀访问的黄华颁发几内亚国家荣誉勋章，表彰他为发展几中友好关系作出的贡献。

November 22,1981. Guinean President Sekou Toure awards a National Medal of Honor to Huang Hua in recognition of his contribution to the development of friendly relations between the two countries.

VII-63 1981年11月25日－28日应邀访问马里共和国。图为马里总统穆萨·特拉奥雷到使馆参加招待会。中间者为外经贸部副部长程飞。

November 25-28,1981. During his visit to Republic of Mali, Huang Hua welcomes President Mousa Traore who attends a reception in the Chinese Embassy.Centre: Deputy-Minister of Foreign Trade Cheng Fei.

VII-64

VII-64　1981年12月4日，加纳总统希拉·利曼博士在阿克拉欢迎来访的黄华。
December 4,1981. President of Ghana Dr. Hilla Limann welcomes Huang Hua in Accra.

VII-65　1981年12月5日，同加纳老朋友会面。
December 5,1981. Huang Hua meets old Ghanaian friends.

VII-65

VII-66 1982年4月27日，在北京钓鱼台国宾馆宴请阿尔及利亚民主人民共和国总统沙德利·本·杰迪德。图为黄华对客人说，两千年前燕国的王子们就在那面的湖边钓鱼。

April 27, 1982. Huang Hua entertains Algerian President Shadli Ben Djedid to a dinner at the Diaoyutai State Guest House in Beijing. Picture shows Huang Hua telling his guests two thousand years ago, the princes of Yan Kingdom went fishing in the lake there.

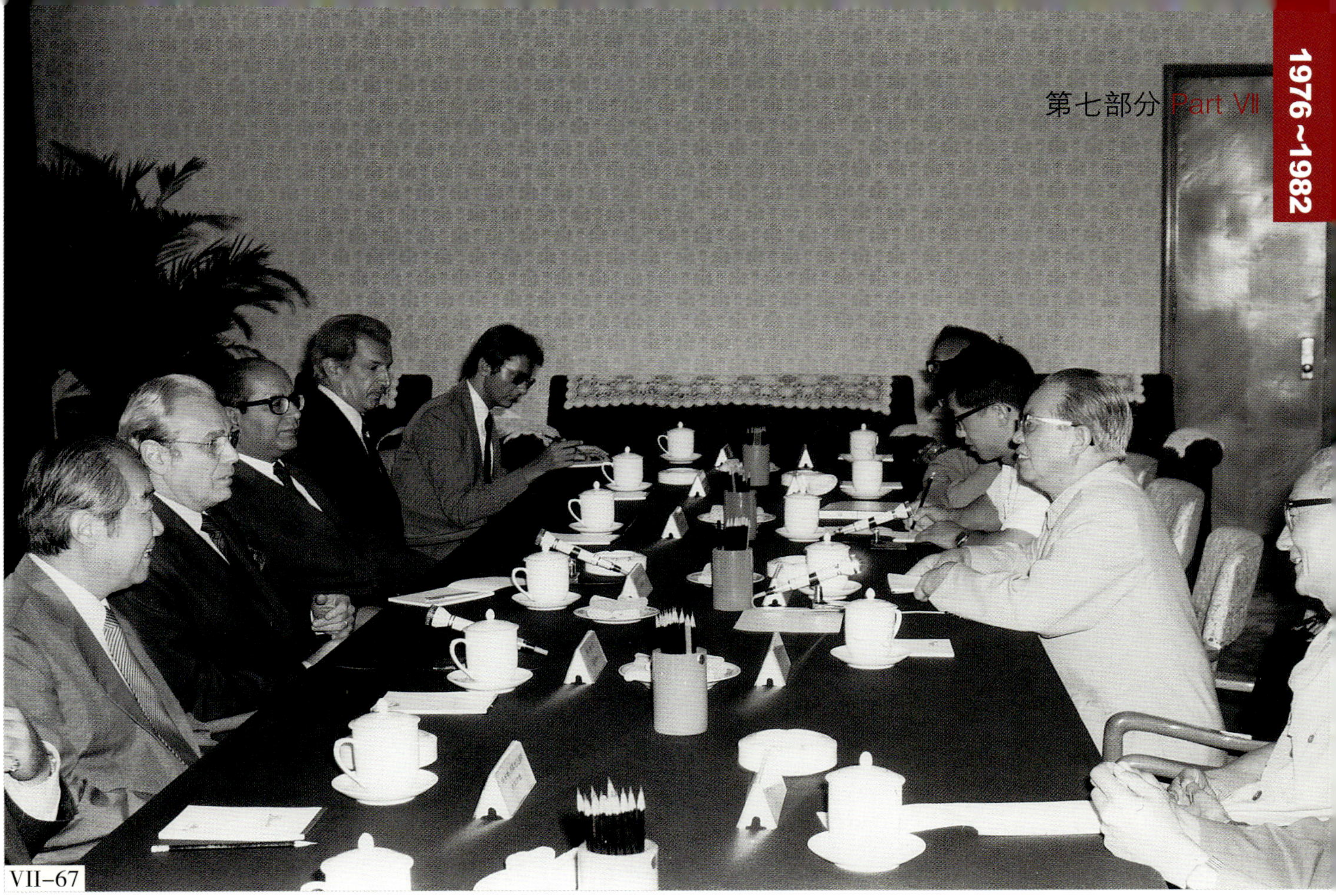

VII–67

VII–67 1982年8月20日，在北京同来访的联合国秘书长佩雷斯·德奎利亚尔会谈。左一为联合国副秘书长毕季龙。
August 20, 1982. Huang Hua holds talks with Perez De Cuellar, UN Secretary General, in Beijing. First left: Bi Jilong, UN Under-Secretary-General.

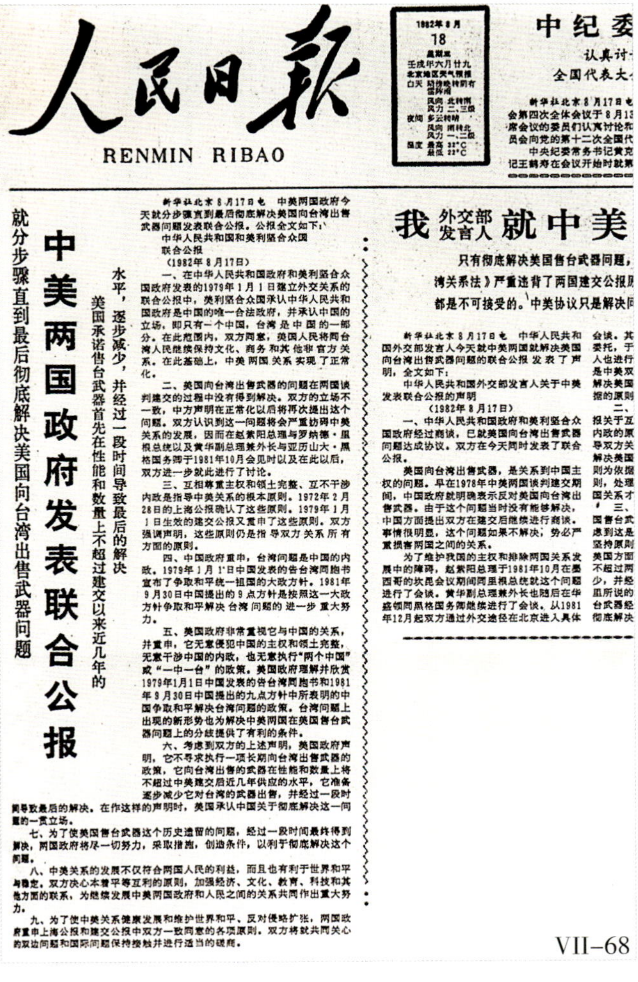

人民日报
RENMIN RIBAO

1982年8月 18 星期三 壬戌年六月廿九

中美两国政府发表联合公报

就分步骤直到最后彻底解决美国向台湾出售武器问题

美国承诺售台武器首先在性能和数量上不超过建交以来近几年的水平，逐步减少，并经过一段时间导致最后的解决

新华社北京8月17日电 中美两国政府今天就分步骤直到最后彻底解决美国向台湾出售武器问题发表联合公报。公报全文如下：

中华人民共和国和美利坚合众国
联合公报
（1982年8月17日）

一、在中华人民共和国政府和美利坚合众国政府发表的1979年1月1日建立外交关系的联合公报中，美利坚合众国承认中华人民共和国政府是中国的唯一合法政府，并承认中国的立场，即只有一个中国，台湾是中国的一部分。在此范围内，双方同意，美国人民将同台湾人民继续保持文化、商务和其他非官方关系。在此基础上，中美两国关系实现了正常化。

二、美国向台湾出售武器的问题在两国谈判建交的过程中没有得到解决。双方的立场不一致，中方声明在正常化以后将再次提出这个问题。双方认识到这一问题将会严重妨碍中美关系的发展，因而在赵紫阳总理与罗纳德·里根总统以及黄华副总理兼外长与亚历山大·黑格国务卿于1981年10月会见时以及在此以后，双方进一步就此进行了讨论。

三、互相尊重主权和领土完整、互不干涉内政是指导中美关系的根本原则。1972年2月28日的上海公报确认了这些原则。1979年1月1日生效的建交公报又重申了这些原则。双方强调声明，这些原则仍是指导双方关系所有方面的原则。

四、中国政府重申，台湾问题是中国的内政。1979年1月1日中国发表的告台湾同胞书宣布了争取和平统一祖国的大政方针。1981年9月30日中国提出的9点方针是按照这一大政方针争取和平解决台湾问题的进一步重大努力。

五、美国政府非常重视它与中国的关系，并重申，它无意侵犯中国的主权和领土完整，无意干涉中国的内政，也无意执行"两个中国"或"一中一台"的政策。美国政府理解并欣赏1979年1月1日中国发表的告台湾同胞书和1981年9月30日中国提出的九点方针中所表明的中国争取和平解决台湾问题的政策。台湾问题上出现的新形势也为解决中美两国在美国售台武器问题上的分歧提供了有利的条件。

六、考虑到双方的上述声明，美国政府声明，它不寻求执行一项长期向台湾出售武器的政策，它向台湾出售的武器在性能和数量上将不超过中美建交后近几年供应的水平，它准备逐步减少它对台湾的武器出售，并经过一段时间导致最后的解决。在作这样的声明时，美国承认中国关于彻底解决这一问题的一贯立场。

七、为了使美国售台武器这个历史遗留的问题，经过一段时间最终得到解决，两国政府将尽一切努力，采取措施，创造条件，以利于彻底解决这个问题。

八、中美关系的发展不仅符合两国人民的利益，而且也有利于世界和平与稳定。双方决心本着平等互利的原则，加强经济、文化、教育、科技和其他方面的联系，为继续发展中美两国政府和人民之间的关系共同作出重大努力。

九、为了使中美关系健康发展和维护世界和平、反对侵略扩张，两国政府重申上海公报和建交公报中双方一致同意的各项原则。双方将就共同关心的双边问题和国际问题保持接触并进行适当的磋商。

我外交部发言人就中美

新华社北京8月17日电 中华人民共和国外交部发言人今天就中美两国就解决美国向台湾出售武器问题的联合公报发表了声明，全文如下：

中华人民共和国外交部发言人关于中美发表联合公报的声明
（1982年8月17日）

一、中华人民共和国政府和美利坚合众国政府经过商谈，已就美国向台湾出售武器问题达成协议。双方在今天同时发表了联合公报。

美国向台湾出售武器，是关系到中国主权的问题。早在1978年中美两国谈判建交期间，中国政府就明确表示反对美国向台湾出售武器。由于这个问题当时没有能够解决，中国方面提出双方在建交后继续进行商谈。事情很明显，这个问题如果不解决，势必严重损害两国之间的关系。

为了维护我国的主权和排除两国关系发展中的障碍，赵紫阳总理于1981年10月在墨西哥的坎昆会议期间同里根总统就这个问题进行了会谈。黄华副总理兼外长也随后在华盛顿同黑格国务卿继续进行了会谈。从1981年12月起双方通过外交途径在北京进入具体

VII–68

VII–68 1982年8月17日，中美两国政府发表关于解决美国售台武器问题的联合公报。
August 17,1982. Governments of China and the United States issue a joint communique on the settlement of the question of U.S. arms sales to Taiwan.

VII-69 1982年9月17日，陪同来访的朝鲜民主主义人民共和国主席金日成向人民英雄纪念碑敬献花圈。
September 17, 1982. Accompanied by Huang Hua, visiting President Kim Il Sung of DPRK lays a wreath at the Monument to the People's Heroes.

VII–70 1982年9月24日，在陪同邓小平与来访的英国首相玛格丽特·撒切尔夫人会谈后，在钓鱼台养源斋宴请撒切尔一行。

September 24, 1982. Accompanied by Huang Hua, Deng Xiaoping holds talks with British Prime Minister Thatcher. After talks, Huang Hua hosts a dinner for Thatcher and her party at the Diaoyutai State Guest House.

VII-71 1982年11月15日，作为中国政府特使在莫斯科红场参加苏联最高苏维埃主席团主席列·伊·勃列日涅夫的葬仪。

November 15,1982. As special envoy of the Chinese government, Huang Hua attends the funeral of Soviet President Leonid Brezhnev in Moscow's Red Square.

VII-72 中国政府特使代表团在莫斯科圆柱大厅参加勃列日涅夫遗体告别式。

The Chinese government delegation pays last respects to the remains of Brezhnev in the Column Hall, Moscow.

VII-73　1982年11月16日，同苏联外长安德烈·葛罗米柯会谈。左二为黄华，左四为杨守正大使，右二为葛罗米柯。
November 16,1982. Huang Hua holds talks with Soviet Foreign Minister Andrei Gromyko. Second left: Huang Hua, fourth left: Ambassador Yang Shouzheng, second right: Gromyko.

VII-74　1982年11月16日，参观苏联加加林宇航中心。
November 16,1982. Huang Hua visits Soviet Gagarin Space Center.

第八部分

任全国人大常委会副委员长和中顾委常委

（1983～1992）

在人大工作期间，除了审议法律文书草案和考察经济与教育发展情况外，黄华还进行了不少外事活动。他率人大代表团出席亚洲议员人口论坛大会，赴坦桑尼亚、赞比亚和拉丁美洲五国访问。他多次出席国际行动理事会年会。在担任中顾委常委期间，黄华用心研究社会主义的经济和社会发展的理论和实践问题，还应邀出席一些国际会议，如里约热内卢联合国环境和发展大会等。

黄华在出访期间，总不忘为中国的革命和建设作出过贡献的老朋友，抽出时间看望他们，转达中国人民对他们的敬意和友情。

Part Eight

Holding office as Vice-Chairman of Standing Committee of National People's Congress and Standing Committee member of CPC Central Advisory Commission

（1983～1992）

During the period when Huang Hua worked in the National People's Congress, he participated in many diplomatic activities in addition to deliberation of drafts of legal documents and investigation into the situation of economic and educational development. He led the delegation of the National People's Congress to attend the Asian Parliamentarian Forum on Population and Development, and visited Tanzania, Zambia and other five countries in Latin America. He attended on several occasions the annual meetings of the Inter-Action Council. In the period when he was a Standing Committee member of CPC Central Advisory Commission, Huang Hua made some in-depth research on theory and practice of socialist economy and social development. He was invited to attend some international conferences, such as UN Conference on Environment and Development in Rio de Janeiro.

During his visit abroad, he never forgot those old friends, who had made contributions to China's revolution and construction, and tried to find time to visit them, conveying to them the respect and friendship of the Chinese people.

VIII-1

VIII-1 1984年12月9日，率全国人大代表团参加坦桑尼亚独立23周年庆典，拜会坦桑尼亚总统朱利叶斯·尼雷尔。

December 9, 1984. Leading a delegation of the National People's Congress (NPC), Huang Hua attends the 23rd anniversary of independence of Tanzania and calls on President Julius Nyerere.

VIII-2

VIII-2 1984年12月16日，率全国人大代表团访问赞比亚，在卢萨卡机场受到鲁宾逊·纳布利雅托议长热情欢迎。中间者为段苏权副团长，右一为辽宁省人大常委会主任张正德。

December 16, 1984. Huang Hua is warmly welcomed by Speaker Mwaake Nabulyato of Zambia at Lusaka airport when he leads a NPC delegation to visit Zambia. Center: Duan Suquan, deputy head of the delegation, first right: Zhang Zhengde, Chairman of the Standing Committee of Liaoning Provincial People's Congress.

VIII-3 1985 年 1 月 16 日，以个人身份应邀赴西班牙巴塞罗那出席国际行动理事会的政策委员会会议。图为同会议成员合影。前排右二为尼日利亚前军政府首脑奥巴桑乔，左三为葡萄牙前总理玛丽亚·平塔西尔戈，右一为黄华。

January 16,1985. Huang Hua attends an Inter-Action Council meeting in a personal capacity in Spain, and has a group photo taken with other participants. Second right in front row: Olusegun Obasanjo, former head of the Nigerian military government, third left: Maria Pintassilgo, former Prime Minister of Portugal, first right: Huang Hua.

VIII-4　1985年6月1日，率全国人大代表团访问委内瑞拉。6月7日在加拉加斯拜会总统海梅·卢辛奇。
June 7,1985. Leading a delegation of the National People's Congress to Venezuela, Huang Hua calls on President Jaime Lucinchi in Caracas.

VIII-5　1985年6月8日，率全国人大代表团访问阿根廷。6月12日在布宜诺斯艾利斯拜会总统阿方辛。
June 12,1985. Leading a NPC delegation to Argentina, Huang Hua calls on President Raul Alfonsin in Buenos Aires.

西安事变五十周年纪念大会
1936—1986

VIII-7

VIII-6　1986年12月，同新西兰作家詹姆士·贝特兰参加全国政协举行的"西安事变"五十周年纪念大会，在主席台上就座。贝特兰是黄华在燕京大学的同宿舍校友。1936年贝特兰在西安用英语广播，使全世界得知"西安事变"的真相。

December 1986. Huang Hua and New Zealand writer James Bertram attend a meeting to commemorate the 50th anniversary of Xi'an Incident. James Bertram was a roommate of Huang Hua in Yenching University. The world learned the truth of the Xi'an Incident from his broadcast in English in December, 1936.

VIII-7　贝特兰于1986年赠给老友王汝梅（黄华）的近照。

A recent photo of James Bertram presented to his old friend Wang Rumei (Huang Hua) in 1986.

VIII-8　1986年10月，在人民大会堂同来访的联合国秘书处非洲司司长顾菊珍和钱家骐博士亲切交谈。

October 1986. A friendly chat with visiting Director of African Affairs of UN Secretariat Patricia Koo Tsien and Dr. K.C. Tsien at the Great Hall of the People.

VIII-8

VIII-9

VIII-9 1987年5月6日，在墨西哥城国民宫拜会墨西哥总统德拉马德里。左一为人大常委委员黄玉昆。
May 6,1987. The Chinese NPC delegation calls on Mexican President Miguel De La Madrid Hurtado. First left: Huang Yukun, member of the Standing Committee of NPC.

VIII-10

VIII-10 1987年5月，率团访问墨西哥。图为中墨两国议员进行会谈。中间者为会谈主持人墨西哥参议院议长安东尼奥·里瓦·巴拉齐奥，中排左一为黄华。
May 1987. Leading a NPC delegation to Mexico, Huang Hua holds talks with Mexican parliamentarians. Antonio Palacio(center), Speaker of the Senate of Mexico, presiding over the talks. First left in middle row: Huang Hua.

VIII-11　1987年5月13日，率全国人大代表团访问哥伦比亚，在波哥大拜访哥伦比亚总统比尔希略·巴尔科·巴尔加斯。

May 13,1987. Leading a NPC delegation to Colombia, Huang Hua calls on Colombian President Virgilio Barco Bargas in Bogota.

VIII-12　1987年5月20日，拜会秘鲁第二副总统兼总理路易斯·阿尔瓦·卡斯特罗。右二为全国人大常委会委员裘维蕃。
May 20,1987. Huang Hua calls on Luis Alva Castro, Second Vice President and Prime Minister of Peru. Second right: Qiu Weifan, Standing Committee member of NPC.

VIII-13

VIII-13 1987年11月，率全国人大代表团访问芬兰。在赫尔辛基拜会芬兰总统毛诺·科伊维斯托。左一为中国驻芬兰大使林霭丽，左二为全国人大常委会委员张承先，右二为黄华。

November 1987. Leading a NPC delegation to Finland, Huang Hua calls on President Mauno Koivisto in Helsinki. First left: Ambassador Lin Aili, second left: Zhang Chengxian, Standing Committee member of NPC, second right: Huang Hua.

VIII-14 "都七老八十的人了，随便坐下来谈谈吧。"1989年5月，出席华盛顿特区年会的国际行动理事会主席、联邦德国前总理赫·施密特对黄华说。

May 1989. Huang Hua attends the annual meeting of the Inter-Action Council in Washington D.C.. Council Chairman and former German Chancellor H.Schmidt says to Huang Hua: "we are old people of late seventies and early eighties, so let's sit down anywhere and have a chat."

VIII-14

VIII–15 1993年5月13日至16日，国际行动理事会第十一届年会在中国上海举行。图为朱镕基副总理同理事会与会者合影。前排左起：弗里泽、刘华秋、卡翁达、平塔西尔戈、黄华、施密特、朱镕基、福田赳夫、黄菊、李光耀、贺光辉、奥巴桑乔、卡拉汉。

From May 13 to 16, 1993. The 11th annual meeting of the Inter- Action Council is held in Shanghai. Vice-Premier Zhu Rongji is photographed with the participants. From left in front row: John Fraser, Liu Huaqiu, Kenneth Kaunda, Maria Pintassilgo, Huang Hua, Schmidt, Zhu Rongji, Takeo Fukuda, Huang Ju, Lee Kuan Yew, He Guanghui, Obasanjo, Callaghan.

开展民间友好交往工作

我国的党和国家领导人一贯重视对国际友人的工作,重视增进中外人民的友谊和理解的工作。

八十年代中,黄华陆续担任五个非政府组织的领导。他们虽然工作侧重点各不相同,但都积极从事国际友好交流活动。

黄华认为,不忘老朋友,广交新朋友的工作十分重要,应该长期继续下去。与老朋友的亲人及后代进行友好交往也不应忽视。

黄华很崇敬慷慨向内地捐资助教的港台和海外爱国人士。

有的民间友好团体经费十分困难,但由于许多志愿工作者的奉献精神,作出了不少成绩,赢得人们的敬重和信赖。黄华经常喜欢与他们交谈,相互鼓励,把工作做得更好。

黄华还同国内外的燕京校友和一二·九运动的战友经常聚会,话忆当年。

Part Nine

Development of Friendly Exchanges Among the People

The leaders of our Party and State always pay attention to working with international friends and promoting friendship and understanding between the Chinese people and people of other countries.

In the middle of the 1980s, Huang Hua held leading positions in five non-governmental organizations in succession. Though they have differences in special emphasis of work, they are all actively engaged in international friendly exchanges.

Huang Hua considers it very important not to forget old friends while making a large circle of new friends. Such work is to be continued over a long period of time. Maintenance of friendly exchanges with family members and descendants of the old friends should not be neglected either.

Huang Hua greatly respects patriots in Hong Kong, Taiwan and abroad, who have made generous contributions to aid students in the mainland.

Some NGOs have encountered financial difficulties, but thanks to the spirit of dedication to work of many volunteer workers, they have achieved great success and won respect and trust of the people. Huang Hua likes to frequently talk with the volunteers and encourage them to perform their work better.

Huang Hua likes to often get together with alumni of Yenching University and comrades-in-arms participating in the December 9th Student Movement, who live at home and abroad, to recall the past.

為各國人民之間的
友誼鋪路架橋

祝賀中國國際友人研究會成立

江澤民

一九九一年三月一日

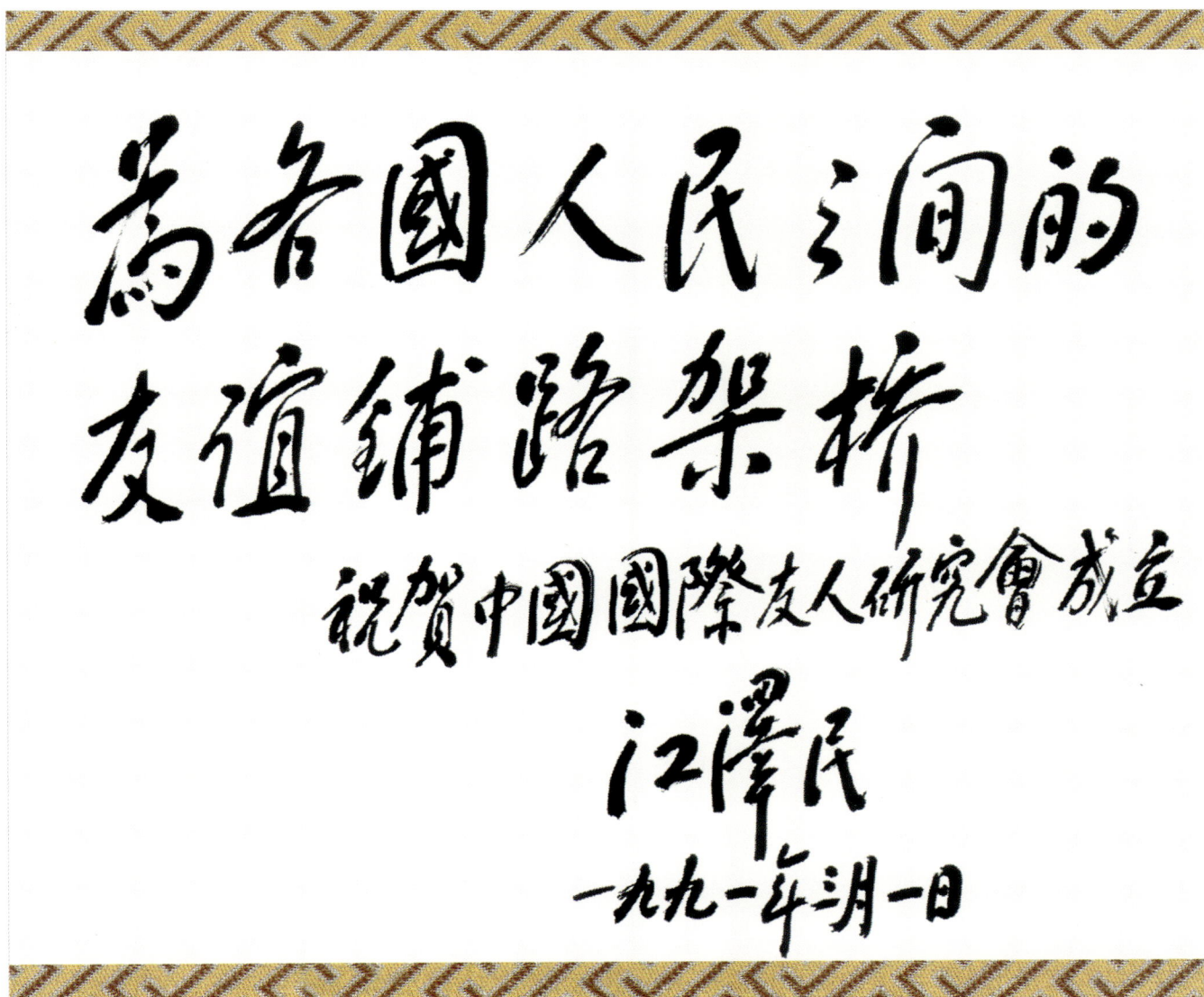

IX-1 1991年3月1日，中国国际友人研究会（前身为斯特朗、史沫特莱、斯诺研究会）成立。黄华任会长。图为江泽民总书记为友研会题词。

March 1,1991. Inscription by General Secretary of CPC Central Committee Jiang Zemin "Paving the road and building bridges to advance the cause of people's friendship" to congratulate the establishment of China Society for People's Friendship Studies (PFS, its predecessor the "Anna Louis Strong, Agnes Smedley and Edgar Snow Society ") , of which Huang Hua was president.

IX-2　1971年7月24日，周恩来会见韩丁、雷洲安、柯弗兰、柯如思、马海德、阳早、寒春等国际友人。第二排右三为黄华。

July 24, 1971. Premier Zhou Enlai meets with foreign friends working in Beijing—William Hinton, Joan Hinton, Frank Coe, Ruth Coe, George Hatem, Erwin Engst and Jone Hinton. Third right in second row: Huang Hua.

IX-3

IX-3 1977年12月2日，出席中国人民对外友好协会为庆祝新西兰作家路易·艾黎八十岁寿辰举行的祝寿宴会。前排左起为：王炳南、廖承志、耿飚、路易·艾黎、邓小平，右一为丁雪松，右三为黄华。

December 2, 1977. A banquet hosted by the Chinese People's Association for Friendship with Foreign Countries to celebrate the 80th birthday of New Zealand writer Rewi Alley. Fourth left in front row: Rewi Alley, fifth left: Deng Xiaoping, first right: Ding Xuesong, third right: Huang Hua.

IX-4　1990 年 6 月 11 日，陪同江泽民总书记在北京人民大会堂会见来访的日本笹川友好基金会名誉会长笹川良一和基金会委员长笹川阳平。右一为黄华。

June 11,1990. Accompanied by Huang Hua, Jiang Zemin, General Secretary of CPC Central Committee, meets with Ryoichi Sasakawa, Honorary Chairman of Sasakawa Friendship Foundation of Japan and Yohei Sasakawa, President of the Foundation at the Great Hall of the People in Beijing. First right: Huang Hua.

IX-5　杨尚昆、黄华、马海德、荣高棠于1983年同美军观察组老友约翰·高林在人民大会堂会面。

1983. Yang Shangkun, Huang Hua, George Hatem, Rong Gaotang meet with John G. Colling, an old friend of the Dixie Mission, at the Great Hall of the People.

IX-6　1991年9月18日，在北京人民大会堂与国家副主席、中国国际友好联络会名誉会长王震，国务院副总理邹家骅同前美军驻延安观察组老朋友赫伯特·希切率领的访华团成员合影。前排右一为黄华，时任友联会会长。

September 18, 1991. Wang Zhen, Vice President of the People's Republic of China and Honorary Chairman of China Association for International Friendly Contact, Zou Jiahua, vice-premier of the State Council, photographed with the visiting group of Dixie Mission led by Herbert Hitch at the Great Hall of the People. First right in front row: Huang Hua, then Chairman of the Association.

IX-7　1972年2月初，斯诺病重，周恩来指示马海德率医疗队去瑞士为他治病。总理又电示在亚的斯亚贝巴出席联合国安全理事会会议的黄华去看望他，并转达他和毛主席的慰问。斯诺在病榻上见到黄华和马海德，兴奋地握住他们的手说："三个赤匪又到一起了！"图为1971年9月玛丽·戴蒙德为斯诺拍摄的最后的照片。

Early February 1972. Edgar Snow is critically ill, Zhou Enlai sends Dr. George Hatem to lead a medical group to Switzerland to treat him. At the same time, the Premier instructs Huang Hua who is attending a UN Security Council session in Addis Abeba to hurry to Switzerland. At the moment Edgar Snow saw Huang Hua, he bursts out in excitement: " The three red bandits are together again!" This is the last photo of Edgar Snow taken by Mary Dimond in September, 1971.

IX-8　1981年8月，同美国斯诺纪念基金会主席玛丽·戴蒙德、E·格雷·戴蒙德大夫、凌青大使一起到纽约市哈德逊河东岸的斯诺纪念石旁拜谒。左一为黄华。

August 1981. Mary Dimond, President of U.S. Edgar Snow Memorial Fund, Dr. E. Grey Dimond and Ambassador Ling Qing pay homage at the memorial stone of Edgar Snow on the eastern bank of Hudson River, New York City. First left: Huang Hua.

IX-9 1985 年 5 月，在美国康涅狄克州同老朋友海伦·斯诺在埃德加·斯诺当年写作的故居里合影。

May 1985. Huang Hua with Helen Snow, an old friend, in the study of Edgar Snow in Connecticut, U.S.A.

IX-10 1992 年 3 月 13 日于北京参加韩素音博士自传首发式。左一为雷洁琼副委员长。

March 13, 1992. At the ceremony celebrating the first publication of Dr. Han Suyin's autobiography. First left: Lei Jieqiong, Vice Chairperson of the Standing Committee of NPC.

IX-11 同参加西班牙反法西斯国际纵队的英国老战士戴维·柯鲁克和夫人伊萨贝尔在柯鲁克夫妇著作首发式上。戴维·柯鲁克于1947年来中国，致力于教育事业五十年。右二为黄华。

At the ceremony celebrating the first publication of the book by David Crook and Isabel Crook. David Crook, a British veteran of the International Brigade against Fascism in Spain, came to China in 1947 and taught English for 50 years. Second right: Huang Hua.

IX-12 1987年3月，在北京同1939年到中国太行山地区抗日前线担任军医的德国医学博士汉斯·米勒合影。自左至右：吴蔚然大夫、马海德大夫、黄华、汉斯·米勒大夫、路易·艾黎。

March 1987. Huang Hua with Hans Muller in Beijing. Hans Muller, a German medical doctor, goes to Anti-Japanese Front in Taihang Mountain Area to serve as a military surgeon in 1939. From left : Dr. Wu Weiran, Dr. George Hatem, Huang Hua, Dr. Hans Muller, Rewi Alley.

146

IX-13　1997年9月，在旧金山老年公寓看望美国友人约翰·谢伟思。
September 1997. Paying a visit to John Service, an American friend, at a home for the aged in San Francisco.

IX-13

IX-14

IX-14　1990年夏，在旧金山与宋庆龄好友和史迪威将军的助手杨孟东（左一）及其夫人海伦合影。
Summer 1990. Huang Hua and He Liliang with Helen and Richard Young (First left) in San Francisco, Richard was a good friend of Soong Ching Ling and assistant to General Joseph.W. Stilwell.

IX-15　1972年夏,于纽约郊区同美国友好人士萨缪·罗森大夫和海伦·罗森合影。右三为海伦·罗森,右二为萨缪·罗森,右一为庄焰大使。
Summer 1972. With American friends Dr. Samuel Rosen and Helen Rosen in the suburbs of New York. Third right: Helen Rosen, second right: Samuel Rosen, first right: Ambassador Zhuang Yan.

IX-16　1997年8月,在北京同来访的美国老朋友比尔·鲍威尔亲切交谈。
August 1997. A cordial chat with visiting American friend Bill Powell in Beijing.

IX-17 1999年9月30日，在国庆五十周年宴会上，同中国人民的老朋友、著名国际社会活动家何鸿章勋爵合影。

September 30, 1999. With Sir Eric Hotung, an old friend of the Chinese people and well-known international social activist, at the banquet to celebrate the 50th anniversary of the founding of People's Republic of China.

IX-18 1985年4月，在英国剑桥拜会英国著名汉学家、中国国际友人研究会名誉顾问、《中国科技史》巨著的作者李约瑟博士。

April 1985. Paying a call on Dr. Joseph Needham, a famous British Sinologist, honorary adviser of PFS and author of the magnum opus Science and Civilization in China, at Cambridge, England.

IX-17

IX-18

IX-19　1999年9月，在北京同中国国际友人研究会的理事和志愿工作者合影。前排自左至右：川越敏孝、寒春、伊萨贝尔·柯鲁克、戴维·柯鲁克、凌青、傅莱大夫、黄华、爱泼斯坦、雪莉·比绍夫、帕特·艾德勒、龚普生、陈必娣、李效黎。

September 1999. With the council members and volunteer workers of the China Society for People's Friendship Studies (PFS) in Beijing. From left in front row: Kawagoe Harudaka,Jone Hinton,Isabel Crook,David Crook,Ling Qing,Dr.Richard Frey, Huang Hua,I.Epstein,Shrill Bishoff,Pat Adler,Gong Pusheng,Betty Chandler,Mrs.Michael Linsey.

IX-20　1973年春，同加拿大友好人士切斯特·朗宁（穰杰德）在北京合影。朗宁是出生在中国的加拿大人，1949年任加拿大驻南京大使馆代办。

Spring 1973. With Chester Ronning, a Canadian friend, in Beijing. Ronning, born in China, was the Charge d'Affaires of Canadian Embassy in Nanjing in 1949.

IX-21　1990年春，在北京同老朋友、《纽约时报》副总编辑西摩·托平及夫人奥德丽（周恩来肖像摄影者）和周文中教授合影。

Spring 1990. With Seymour Topping, Deputy Editor-in-Chief of *New York Times,* and Audrey Topping (Photographer of Zhou Enlai's portrait) and Professor Zhou Wenzhong in Beijing.

IX-22　1997年5月，与龚普生专程赴美国康涅狄克州麦迪逊市参加中国人民的老朋友海伦·福斯特·斯诺的葬仪，同驻美使馆外交官在海伦的灵柩前合影。左二为李道豫大使，左四为龚普生大使，右三为邱胜云总领事，右二为顾品锷副总领事，左三为黄华。

May 1997. Making a special trip with Gong Pusheng to Madison, Connecticut, U.S.A., Huang Hua attends the funeral of Helen Foster Snow, an old friend of Chinese people. Photo taken beside the coffin of Helen Snow with diplomats of Chinese Missions in U.S. Second left: Ambassador Li Daoyu, fourth left: Ambassador Gong Pusheng, third right: Qiu Shengyun, Consul General, second right: Gu Pin'e, Deputy Consul General, third left: Huang Hua.

IX-23　1997年5月2日，在麦迪逊市举行的海伦·斯诺追悼会上致悼词。左一为海伦的侄女雪莉·比绍夫，一位执著地为中美人民友好和理解努力工作的架桥人。

May 2, 1997. Giving a speech at the memorial meeting for Helen Snow at Madison, Connecticut. First left: Shirley Bishoff, Helen's niece, who works hard to persist in playing the role of a bridge of friendship and understanding between the Chinese and American peoples.

IX-24 1997年12月，应新西兰亚洲2000年基金会邀请，出席克赖斯特彻奇市纪念路易·艾黎的集会并讲话。前排右三为新西兰总督波依斯，右二为波依斯夫人。

December 1997. Invited by New Zealand Asia 2000 Foundation, Huang Hua attends the memorial meeting for Rewi Alley in Christchurch and delivers a speech. Third right in front row : Michael Hardie Boys, Governor General of New Zealand, second right: Lady Boys.

IX-25 1997年12月，于奥克兰同竖立在艾黎妹妹乔伊斯花园里的艾黎塑像对话。

December 1997. Talking to the bust of Rewi Alley in the garden of Rewi's sister Joyce Alley in Auckland.

IX-26　1985年5月12日，在北京同日本老朋友西园寺公一和夫人合影。后排左起为：王效贤、何理良、黄华、西园寺公一、雪江夫人。

May 12, 1985. With Japanese old friend Kinkazu Saionji and Madame Saionji. From left in back row: Wang Xiaoxian, He Liliang, Huang Hua, Kinkazu Saionji, Madame Saionji.

IX-27 　2000 年 10 月，在北京会见日本前首相村山富市。
October 2000. Meeting with former Japanese Prime Minister Tomiichi Murayama in Beijing.

IX-28 　2002 年 9 月，于北京同日中友协会长、日本著名画家平山郁夫合影。
September 2002. At a dinner in Beijing with Ikuo Hirayama, President of Japan-China Friendship Association and famous Japanese painter .

IX-29

IX-29　以宋庆龄基金会主席身份在东京拜会宋庆龄日本基金会会长宇都宫德马（前排右二）。前排左一为秘书长久保田博子，左二为理事长武田清子教授，前排右一为黄华。As Chairman of the Soong Ching Ling Foundation, Huang Hua pays a visit in Tokyo to Tokuma Utsunomiya, Chairman of the Soong Ching Ling Foundation of Japan (second right in front row). First left in front row: Hiroko Kubota, second left: Professor Kiyoko Takeda, first right in front row: Huang Hua.

IX-30

IX-30　1997年9月28日，在北京人民大会堂同日本朋友清水正夫和南村志郎合影。左二为唐家璇，右一为齐怀远。中间者为黄华。
September 28, 1997. With Japanese friends Masao Shimizu and Shiro Minamimura at the Great Hall of the People in Beijing. Second left: Tang Jiaxuan, first right: Qi Huaiyuan, center: Huang Hua.

IX-31 同热情为中日人民友好和理解而工作的日本知名人士园田天光光合影。
With Tenkoko Sonoda, a Japanese celebrity who enthusiastically works for people's friendship and understanding between China and Japan.

IX-32 1989年5月，在北京会见第一百次访华的日本经济界老朋友、日中经济协会常任顾问冈崎嘉平太。
May 1989. Meeting in Beijing with Kaheita Okazaki, a Japanese old friend in economic circle and permanent advisor of the Japan-China Economic Association, on his 100th visit to China.

IX-33 同香港知名实业家包玉刚和日本友好人士木村一三合影。前排左二为木村一三，左三为包玉刚，右二为黄华。

With Y.K. Pao, a famous industrialist in Hong Kong, and Japanese friend Kazuzo Kimura. Second left in front row: Kazuzo Kimura, third left: Y.K. Pao, second right: Huang Hua.

IX-34 同尊重中日关系历史事实和教育孩子们不说假话的日本中小学教师合影。前排左二为黄华。左三为大田尧先生。

With teachers of Japanese primary and middle schools. They come to China to learn the true historical facts of Japan-China relations and teach students never to tell lies. Second left in front row: Huang Hua.

IX-35

IX-35　1984年4月16日，在家中会见44年前在延安学习的日本朋友。左四为延安对日工作干部学校的日语教员王艾英，右四为黄华。

April 16, 1984. At home, Huang Hua meets the Japanese friends who studied in Yan'an 44 years ago. Fourth left: Wang Aiying, a teacher of the school of Japanese language in Yan'an, fourth right: Huang Hua.

IX-36

IX-36　2002年5月，前田先生把18年前黄华在同日本朋友会见时书赠的鲁迅诗句送至北京以补盖名章。

编者注：黄华已向友人声明："相逢"误写为"相见"。

May 2002. The son of Mr. Maeda comes to Beijing and asks Huang Hua to affix his personal seal to the calligraphy with quotation of a famous poem of Lu Xun written at the meeting with the Japanese friends 18 years ago.

IX-37 同孙中山的日本好友梅屋庄吉之孙女小坂主和子及其丈夫小坂哲瑯合影。他们都是为中日人民友谊热情工作的朋友。

With Shiuwako Kosaka, granddaughter of Shokichi Wumeya, and her husband Tetturou kosaka, friends working enthusiastically for friendship between the peoples of Japan and China. Shokichi Wumeya is a good friend of Dr. Sun Yat-sen.

IX-38 孙中山的日本好友梅屋庄吉于1933年将孙中山纪念铜像赠给中国，被放在广州中山大学校园内。图为2003年1月黄华在铜像前留影。王景堂摄。

The bronze statue of Dr. Sun Yat-sen donated to China by Shokichi Wumeya in 1933, was erected in the campus of Zhongshan University in Guangzhou. Picture shows Huang Hua standing in front of the statue in January 2003. *Photo by Wang Jingtang.*

IX-39

IX-39　1985年4月，美国埃德加·斯诺图书馆在堪萨斯城正式开放，黄华出席。密苏里州堪萨斯城大学终身教授、斯诺纪念基金主席戴蒙德博士主持剪彩仪式。

April 1985. Huang Hua attends the opening ceremony of the U.S. Edgar Snow Library in Kansas City. Dr. E. Grey Dimond, Professor of the University of Missouri Kansas City and Chairman of U.S. Edgar Snow Memorial Fund presiding over the ribbon-cutting ceremony.

IX-40

IX-40　1985年4月，密苏里州堪萨斯城大学授予"三S"研究会会长黄华名誉文学博士衔。前排左一为黄华。

April 1985. The University of Missouri Kansas City awards Huang Hua, President of the "Strong, Smedley, Snow Society", an honorary doctorate. First left in front row: Huang Hua.

IX-41 2000年10月，第九届斯诺研讨会和纪念斯诺画展在北京举行。以戴蒙德博士为团长、念希·威尔逊为副团长的斯诺纪念基金代表团出席。图为在画展上。左一为余建亭顾问，左二为凌青副会长，右一为黄华。

October 2000. The 9th Edgar Snow Symposium and an art exhibition in memory of Edgar Snow are held in Beijing. A delegation of U.S. Edgar Snow Memorial Fund led by Dr. E. Grey Dimond and Nancy Wilson attending the exhibition. First left: Yu Jianting, Advisor of PFS, second left: Ling Qing, Vice President of PFS, first right: Huang Hua.

IX-42 1995年6月，同来访的中国国际友人研究会名誉理事、美国友人戴维·杜波依斯在家里合影。

June 1995. With visiting American friend David Du Bois, honorary council member of PFS in Beijing.

162

IX-43　1990 年秋，于重庆在史迪威研讨会上同史迪威将军的女儿南希·伊斯特布鲁克合影。

Autumn 1990. With Nancy Easterbrook, daughter of General J. W. Stilwell at Stilwell Symposium in Chongqing.

IX-44　1991 年 2 月，于美国加州弗列斯诺市同热情帮助中国发展的美国著名畜牧专家玛里恩·E·恩斯明格博士及夫人合影。

February 1991. With Dr. Marion E. Ensminger, a well-known American expert on animal husbandry, and Mrs. Ensminger in Flesnorth, California. Dr. Ensminger is energetic in promoting China's development in the field.

IX-45 1994年7月，在上海体育馆参加中国福利会举办的首届国际少年儿童文化艺术节开幕式。第二排左三为吴邦国，左四为黄华，左五为黄菊，左六为陈至立。

July 1994. The opening ceremony of the First Youth and Children Cultural and Art Festival sponsored by the China Welfare Institute at the Shanghai Gymnasium. Third left in second row: Wu Bangguo, fourth left: Huang Hua, fifth left: Huang Ju, sixth left: Chen Zhili.

IX-46 1998年6月，在香港华润大厦参加宋庆龄在香港创立的保卫中国同盟（后改名为中国福利会）建立六十周年纪念会。香港特首董建华(右二)、外交部驻港特派员马毓真（右一）、驻香港新华分社副社长朱育诚（左一）应邀出席。右三为黄华。
June 1998. Participating in the commemoration meeting of the 60th anniversary of China Defence League (later renamed China Welfare Institute) established by Soong Ching Ling in Hong Kong, which is held in Hong Kong China Resources Building, are: Tung Chee Hwa, Chief Executive of Hong Kong Special Administrative Region (HKSAR); Ma Yuzhen, Commissioner of the Ministry of Foreign Affairs in HKSAR. Zhu Yucheng, Deputy Director,Xinhua News Agency in HKSAR. Third right: Huang Hua.

IX-47 1986年3月6日，在上海祝贺九十岁华诞的中国福利会顾问、美籍专家耿丽淑。
March 6, 1986. Congratulating Talithe Gerlach, advisor of China Welfare Institute and an American expert, on her 90th birthday in Shanghai.

IX-48 1994 年 10 月，同中国福利会的战友们访问海南省文昌市宋庆龄纪念馆。自左至右为：梁于藩、鲁平、黄华、爱泼斯坦、李储文、许德馨各位副主席。

October 1994. With veteran members of the China Welfare Institute visiting the Soong Ching Ling Memorial House in Wenchang City of Hainan Province. From left: Liang Yufan, Lu Ping, Huang Hua, Israel Epstein, Li Chuwen, Xu Dexin, all being Vice Chairmen of the Institute.

IX-49 1995 年 4 月 22 日，在上海向中国福利会赴安徽金寨服务团授旗。

April 22, 1995 in Shanghai. Presenting a flag to the service group organized by the China Welfare Institute to go to Jinzhai, Anhui Province.

IX-50　1994 年 10 月 1 日国庆节，在北京同中国福利会少年宫赴京表演团小演员们合影。
With young performers from Shanghai Children's Palace of the China Welfare Institute in Beijing on the National Day of October 1st 1994.

IX-51　在与国外少年儿童进行文化交流中，中国福利会的小伙伴艺术团十分活跃。图为 1995 年 11 月 1 日，同在韩国访问的小伙伴艺术团的孩子们合影。
November 1, 1995. Huang Hua with members of the Little Companion Art Troupe of the China Welfare Institute, who are visiting the Republic of Korea.

IX-52　1996 年 5 月 29 日，于北京宋庆龄故居同全国政协副主席钱正英在宋庆龄雕像揭幕式上合影。

May 29, 1996. With Qian Zhengying, Vice Chairperson of the National Committee of the Chinese People's Political Consultative Conference, at the unveiling ceremony of Soong Ching Ling's bust in the former residence of Soong Ching Ling in Beijing.

IX-53　1993 年 1 月，时为宋庆龄基金会主席的黄华在北京纪念宋庆龄诞辰一百周年纪念会上，同雷洁琼副委员长和宋庆龄基金会香港理事林贝聿嘉女士合影。

January 1993. With Lei Jieqiong, Vice Chairperson of the Standing Committee of the National People's Congress, and Ms. Peggy Pei Lam, Hong Kong council member of the Soong Ching Ling Foundation, at the centenary of the birth of Soong Ching Ling in Beijing. Huang Hua is Chairman of the Foundation.

IX-54　1993年9月17日，同香港律政司司长梁爱诗合影。
September 17, 1993. With Elsie Oi-sie Leung, Secretary for Justice of Hong Kong.

IX-55　1993年1月，同宋庆龄基金会名誉理事、孙中山的后人孙治强合影。
January 1993. With T. K. Sun, honorary council member of the Soong Ching Ling Foundation and a grandson of Dr. Sun Yat-sen.

IX-56　1993年10月4日，陪同第十一次访华的南方委员会主席朱利叶斯·尼雷尔在宋庆龄故居参观宋庆龄生平事迹展览。

October 4, 1993. Accompanying Julius K. Nyerere, Chairman of the Southern Commission, to visit the exhibition of Soong Ching Ling's life story at the former residence of Soong Ching Ling during J.K.Nyerere's 11th trip to China.

IX-57　1994年10月14日，在东京举行宋庆龄基金会和宋庆龄日本基金会第五次联席会议。图为与会者合影。前排左五为武田清子，右五为黄华，右一为久保田博子。

October 14, 1994. The 5th China-Japan Joint Meeting of the Soong Ching Ling Foundation in Tokyo. Fifth left in front row: Kiyoko Takeda, fifth right: Huang Hua, first right: Hiroko Kubota.

IX–58　2000年10月，在北京出席宋庆龄基金会第二届"孙平化日本学学术奖励基金"颁奖仪式。左一为俞贵麟，左三为周铁农，左四为村山富市，左五为罗豪才，右五为黄华，右四为平山郁夫，右三为刘德有。

October 2000. Attending the Prize-Giving Ceremony of the Second "Sun Pinghua Fund for Japanology Award" of the Soong Ching Ling Foundation in Beijing. First left: Yu Guilin, third left: Zhou Tienong, Fourth left: Tomiichi Murayama, former, fifth left: Luo Haocai, fifth right: Huang Hua, fourth right: Ikuo Hirayama, President of the Japan-China Friendship Association, third right: Liu Deyou.

IX–59　日本狮子会东京330A地区的主席小坂哲瑯是宋庆龄基金会名誉理事。狮子会会员们对宁夏的扶贫助教项目慷慨捐赠，并邀请宁夏的小学生到东京参观。图为2001年5月，黄华和小学生们出席该会大会的情况。左二为小坂哲瑯。

Tetturou Kosaka, Chairman of the 330-A District (Tokyo) of the LIONS Club International and honorary council member of the Soong Ching Ling Foundation. The LIONS Club International contributes generously to help the poor and education in Ningxia Hui Autonomous Region and also invites students from Ningxia to visit Tokyo. Picture shows Huang Hua and students taking part in a meeting organized by the club in May 2001. Second left: Tetturou Kosaka.

IX-60　1998年5月，陪同宋庆龄基金会名誉理事陈志昆(后排右二)和黄寿珍(后排右一)到河北丰宁县向大滩小学热情捐款建校。图为同孩子们合影。后排左二为黄华。

May 1998. Accompanying Walter Chee Kwon Chun and Sau Dhun Wong, honorary council members of the Soong Ching Ling Foundation, on a visit to the Datan Primary School in Fengning County, Hebei Province. They make contributions to build the school. Second left in back row: Huang Hua.

IX-61　1999年10月，同大力推动香港妇女儿童了解祖国历史、社会和文化的宋庆龄基金会理事伍淑清合影。右二为黄华，右三为全国政协副主席孙孚凌，右四为伍淑清，右五为爱泼斯坦，左五为全国政协副主席钱伟长。

October 1999. With Annie Wu, council member of the Soong Ching Ling Foundation, who actively teaches women and children in Hong Kong about the history, society and culture of the motherland. Second right: Huang Hua, third right: Sun Fuling, Vice Chairman of the Chinese People's Political Consultative Conference National Committee, fourth right: Annie Wu, fifth right: Israel Epstein, fifth left: Qian Weichang, Vice Chairman of CPPCC National Committee.

172

IX-62 2000年,同台湾少年儿童访问团团长李钟桂博士在联欢会上。

2000. With Dr. C. K. Lee, leader of the Visiting Group of Taiwan Youth and Children, at a get-together.

IX-63 在北京宋庆龄故居前同台湾顶新集团代表团合影。前排左二为林丽韫,左三为黄华,左四为全国政协副主席程思远。

With the delegation of the Ting Hsin Group from Taiwan in front of the former residence of Soong Ching Ling. Second left in front row: Lin Liyun, third left: Huang Hua, fourth left: Cheng Siyuan, Vice Chairman of the National Committee of CPPCC.

IX-64 2002年5月，在北京出席宋庆龄基金会成立20周年纪念大会。前排左起分别为林佳楣、何振梁、伍绍祖、荣高棠、黄华、王兆国、吴仪、何鲁丽、胡启立、倪志福、王光美、鲁平、刘延东、汪志敏。

IX-64

May 2002. At the commemoration meeting of the 20th anniversary of the establishment of the Soong Ching Ling Foundation in Beijing. From left in front row: Lin Jiamei, He Zhenliang, Wu Shaozu, Rong Gaotang, Huang Hua, Wang Zhaoguo, Wu Yi, He Luli, Hu Qili, Ni Zhifu, Wang Guangmei, Lu Ping, Liu Yandong and Wang Zhimin.

IX-65 1995年10月，于黄山同美国宋庆龄基金会发起人陈志昆及夫人合影。中间者为黄华。
October 1995 on Huangshan Mountain. With Mister and Mrs. Chi Kun Chen, President of the Soong Ching Ling Foundation in America. Center: Huang Hua.

IX-66 1999年10月，同匈牙利宋庆龄儿童友好基金会主席伍德瓦里·卡博尔合影。左一为温业湛，左二为黄华。
October 1999. With Gabor Udvari, Director of the Soong Ching Ling Hungarian Children Friendship Foundation. First left: Wen Yezhan, second left: Huang Hua.

IX-67 1993年12月，以中国国际友好联络会会长身份于曼谷拜会泰国前外长、时任枢密院大臣的西提·沙卫西拉空军上将。

December 1993 in Bangkok. Huang Hua, Chairman of the China Association for International Friendly Contact, calls on H.E. Air Chief Marshal Siddhi Savetsila, Privy Councilor and former Minister of Foreign Affairs of Thailand.

IX-68 1993年12月4日，与泰国副总理兼内政部长、泰中文化经济协会会长差瓦立·永猜育上将共同主持曼谷唐人街华人庆祝国王寿辰的盛大活动。

December 4,1993. General Chavalit Yongchaiyudh, Vice Premier, Interior Minister and President of Thai-China Cultural and Economic Association, and Huang Hua jointly preside over a grand event organized by people in Chinatown, Bangkok, in celebration of the King's birthday.

IX-69 1993年12月，于曼谷拜会泰中文化经济协会副会长帕·阿卡尼布上将。
December 1993. Meeting with General Pat Akkanibut, Vice President of the Thai-China Cultural and Economic Association in Bangkok.

IX-70 1994年6月，于曼谷同正大集团董事长谢国民（前排左六）及夫人（前排左五）合影。右六为黄华，右五何理良，右四王俊夫。
June 1994. With Dhanin Chearawanont, Chairman of C. P. Group of Thailand, and Mrs.D.Chearawanont in Bangkok. Sixth right: Huang Hua,fifth right:He Liliang,fourth right:Wang Junfu.

IX-71　1990 年 12 月，应邀访问日本，拜会日本首相海部俊树。December 1990. Invited to visit Japan, Huang Hua calls on Toshiki Kaifu, Japanese Prime Minister.

IX-72　1992 年 11 月 16 日，与叶选平率中国友好代表团访问日本。图为在东京与日本朋友合影。前排左起为：叶选平、黄华、笹川良一、宋之光。

November 16, 1992. Huang Hua leads a goodwill mission on a visit to Japan. Photo taken with Japanese friends in Tokyo. From left in front row: Ye Xuanping, Huang Hua, Ryoichi Sasakawa, Song Zhiguang.

IX-73　1992 年 11 月 18日，在东京拜会日本首相宫泽喜一。
November 18, 1992. Paying an official call on Kiichi Miyazawa, Japanese Prime Minister, in Tokyo.

IX-74　1993年10月，在东京福田事务所同日本前首相福田赳夫、佐藤隆、笹川阳平、福田康夫合影。左三为黄华。
October 1993. With Takeo Fukuda, former Japanese Prime Minister, Takashi Sato, Yohei Sasakawa, Yasuo Fukuda in the office of Fukuda in Tokyo. Third left: Huang Hua.

IX-75 1992年11月，应邀访问日本。图为日本前代理首相伊东正义及夫人设宴亲切招待黄华及夫人。后排右二右三为杨振亚大使及夫人，右一为伊东正义之侄女。

November 1992. During Huang Hua visit to Japan, Masayoshi Ito, former acting Prime Minister of Japan, and Mrs. lto give a banquet in honor of Huang Hua and He Liliang. Second right in back row: Ambassador Yang Zhenya, first right: niece of Masayoshi Ito.

IX-76 1998年9月，同友联会副会长们在东京拜会日本前首相村山富市。自左至右：陈华、黄华、村山富市、梁湜、邓榕。

September 1998. Huang Hua and other Vice Chairmen of the China Association for International Friendly Contact call on Tomiichi Murayama, former Japanese Prime Minister. From left: Chen Hua, Huang Hua, Tomiichi Murayama, Liang Shi and Deng Rong.

IX-77　1994 年春，应俄罗斯驻华大使罗高寿邀请到俄罗斯驻华大使馆做客。

Spring 1994. Huang Hua is invited by Igor Rogachev, Russian Ambassador to China, to be a guest in the Russian Embassy.

IX-78　1985 年 5 月，应邀访问美国。图为在亚特兰大同哈盖依博士和前美国常驻联合国代表安德鲁·扬合影。

May 1985. Invited to visit the U.S., Huang Hua is photographed with Dr. Edmond Haggai and Andrew Young, former U.S. representative to the U.N., in Atlanta.

IX-79　1991 年 1 月 23 日访问美国期间，应布什总统邀请到白宫叙谈。

January 23, 1991. During his visit to the U.S., Huang Hua is invited by President Bush to have a chat in the White House.

IX-80　2006 年 10 月，在北京同基辛格博士会见。

October 2006. Meets with Dr. Kissinger in Beijing.

IX-81　1997年7月，在北京人民大会堂，以中国国际友好联络会会长身份向汤加国王陶法阿豪·图普四世赠送铜像。左起：程允贤（塑像作者）、王后、国王、黄华、公主、何理良、岳枫、张文朴。

July 1997. As Chairman of China Association for International Friendly Contact, Huang Hua presents a bronze statue to Taufa' Ahau Tupou IV, King of Tonga, in the Great Hall of the People in Beijing. From left: Cheng Yunxian (sculptor), the Queen of Tonga, the King, Huang Hua, Princess, He Liliang, Yue Feng and Zhang Wenpu.

IX-82 1997年3月，在新德里访问拉吉夫·甘地纪念基金会会长索尼亚·甘地夫人。前排左一为中国国际友好联络会副会长王俊夫。

March 1997. Paying a visit to Mrs. Sonia Gandhi, Chairperson of Rajiv Gandhi Memorial Foundation in New Delhi, India. First left in front row: Wang Junfu, Vice Chairman of China Association for International Friendly Contact.

IX–83　1992年9月14日，访问韩国，在汉城青瓦台拜会韩国总统卢泰愚。

September 14, 1992. Calling on Roh Tae Woo, President of the Republic of Korea, in Chong Wa Dae, Seoul.

IX–84　1994年11月，访问韩国汉城期间，在东亚日报社题字留念。右二为东亚日报社长金炳官。

November 1994. Huang Hua's calligraphy written for the Donga Ilbo in Seoul, Republic of Korea. Second right: Kim Byoung-kwan, President of Donga Ilbo.

186

IX-85　1993 年 9 月20日，于北京同韩中友协会长朴晟容合影。

September 20, 1993. With Park Seong Yong, President of Korea-China Friendship Association, in Beijing.

IX-86　1992 年 9 月，在庆州同韩国友好人士张致赫及夫人合影。

September 1992. With friends from the Republic of Korea. Chang Chi Hyeok and Mrs. Chang in Kyong Joo.

IX-87 1990 年 10 月 6 日，在长达五万公里的中国长城的东端的山海关城墙上同长城学会的几位领导人合影。左二为侯仁之，左三为杨国宇，左四为黄华，正中为王定国，右三为罗哲文。

October 6, 1990. With colleagues of the Great Wall Society at the Shanhaiguan Pass at the east end of the 50,000-kilometer Great Wall. Second left: Hou Renzhi, third left: Yang Guoyu, fourth left: Huang Hua, center: Wang Dingguo, third right: Luo Zhewen.

IX-87

IX-88

IX-88 1994 年 10 月，于北京在长城学术研讨会上讲话。右起为：严济慈、雷洁琼、黄华、清水正夫、张德勤。
October 1994. Speaking at the Great Wall Symposium in Beijing. From right: Yan Jici, Lei Jieqiong, Huang Hua, Masao Shimizu, Zhang Deqin.

IX-89   2001 年 7 月，长城学会会长黄华和同事们在北京八达岭长城上合影。前排左二为董耀会,左三为张振,左四为黄华。

July 2001. Huang Hua, Chairman of the Great Wall Society, with colleagues of the Society at Badaling Section of the Great Wall. Second left in front row: Dong Yaohui, third left: Zhang Zhen, fourth left: Huang Hua.

IX-90   1992 年 8 月 24 日，在位于甘肃省的长城嘉峪关城楼上同外国游人交谈。

August 24, 1992. Talking with foreign tourists on Jiayuguan Pass of the Great Wall in Gansu Province.

IX-91　1999年6月,以中山大学岭南学院董事会名誉主席名义同热心支持祖国大学教育的董事们合影。
自左至右为:伍沾德、伍舜德、黄华、叶葆定、黄炳礼、林植宣。

June 1999. Huang Hua, in his capacity as Honorary Chairman, posing for a group photo with board of trustees members of the Lingnam College of Sun Yat-sen University. They enthusiastically support university education of the motherland. From left: Dr. James T. Wu, Professor S.T. Wu, Huang Hua, Professor Ip Po Ting, Dr. Bing Lai Wong and Dr. Chik Suen Lam.

IX-92　1999年6月,在广州同生活节俭但慷慨捐款助学的岭南学院董事、九十一岁的加拿大籍华人叶葆定老先生合影。

June 1999 in Guangzhou. With Professor Ip Po Ting, 91-year-old board member of the Lingnam College and a Chinese-Canadian. Professor Ip has made generous contributions to aid students, but lives a very frugal life himself.

IX-93　1999年6月，在广州中山大学岭南学院同麻省理工学院斯隆管理学院合作仪式上合影。自左至右:黄炳礼博士、莱萨德教授、郭志权博士、叶葆定教授、怀特教授、黄华、林植宣博士、伍沾德博士、舒元博士、戴兰荪博士。

June 1999. Group photo at the ceremony of cooperation between the Sloong School of Management of Massachusetts Institute of Technology and Lingnam College of Sun Yat-sen University in Guangzhou. From left: Dr. Bin Lai Wong, Professor Donald Lessard, Dr. Fillips Kwok, Professor Ip Po Ting, Professor Alan White, Huang Hua, Dr. Chik Suen Lam, Dr. James T. Wu, Dr. Shu Yuan, Dr. L.S. Dai.

IX-94　同岭南学院董事会董事、香港商务印书馆董事总经理兼总编辑陈万雄合影。

With Chan Man-Hung, board member of the Lingnam College as well as Managing Director and Chief Editor of the Commercial Press (Hong Kong).

IX-95　同以"作育英才"为办校宗旨的岭南学人合影。前排左六为王珣章教授，右一为邹至庄教授，右二为道格拉斯·默莱教授，右六为黄华。中排左七为黄焕秋教授，右五为王仲芳教授。后排右七为陆建源博士，右一为陈乐义教授。

Huang Hua with scholars of Lingnam College of Sun Yat-sen University. The purpose of running the College is to foster talents. Sixth left in front row: Professor Wang Xunzhang, first right: Professor Gregory Chow, second right: Professor Douglas Murray, sixth right: Huang Hua, seventh left in second row: Professor Huang Huanqiu, fifth right: Professor Wang Zhongfang, seventh right in third row: Dr. K. Y. Luk, first right: Dr. Loyi Chan.

IX-96　1999年1月，同海南开发促进会的同志合影。前排自左至右：胡昭衡、钱信忠、黄华、于光远、李昌、朱厚泽。

January 1999. With members of the Hainan Development Promotion Association. From left in front row: Hu Zhaoheng, Qian Xinzhong, Huang Hua, Yu Guangyuan, Li Chang and Zhu Houze.

IX-97　1999年1月,同海南开发促进会副理事长于光远、海南省委书记杜青林亲切交谈。

January 1999 in Haikou city, Hainan. A cordial talk with Yu Guangyuan, Vice President of the Hainan Development Promotion Association, and Du Qinglin, Secretary of the Hainan Provincial Committee of CPC.

IX-97

IX-98

IX-98　1997年5月,同燕京大学校友在洛杉矶聚会。前排左起为:刘金定、黄华、谢国振、何理良、杨敏、杨富森。
May 1997. With alumni of Yenching University in LosAngeles. From left in front row: Liu Jinding,Huang Hua,Kuo-Cheng Hsieh,He Liliang,Yang Min,Fu-Shen Yang.

IX-99

IX-99　1989年4月，在北京大学临湖轩前同前燕京大学校友为庆祝母校建立七十周年聚会合影。

April 1989. A get-together of alumni of Yenching University to celebrate the 70th anniversary of the founding of the University, in front of Linhuxuan House, Peking University.

IX-100

IX-100　燕大校友肖成大先生和刘季成大夫于1987年5月率夏威夷心脏外科医疗组来北京做示范手术。图为同医疗组成员在北京中山公园合影。前排右一为黄华。

May 1987. With members of the cardiac surgery team from Hawaii led by Yenching University alumni Mr. Sung Dai Seu and Dr. Edward K. Lau, in Zhongshan Park in Beijing. The team has come to perform demonstration surgery to Chinese doctors. First right in front row: Huang Hua.

IX-101 2000年12月在北京出席纪念一二·九运动六十五周年座谈会。自右起：余建亭、黄华、孟英、陆璀、吴承明、张洁珣、靳明、周强。

December 2000. Attending a forum in Beijing in commemoration of the 65th anniversary of the December 9th Student Movement. From right: Yu Jianting, Huang Hua, Meng Ying, Lu Cui, Wu Chengming, Zhang Jiexun, Jin Ming, Zhou Qiang.

IX-102 2000年12月6日，同参加燕京大学一二·九运动的战友在北京聚首合影。前排左起：郑文、汪溪、黄华、靳明、张韵斐、吴青、孙以芳、杜若、李植人。后排左起：张勉学、朱启明、柯华、刘家栋、高霭亭、余建亭、倪明、陈浩、王若林、魏莲一。

December 6, 2000. A gathering with Yenching University alumni taking part in the December 9th Student Movement in Beijing. From left in front row: Zheng Wen, Wang Xi, Huang Hua, Jin Ming, Zhang Yunfei, Wu Qing, Sun Yifang, Du Ruo, Li Zhiren. From left back row: Zhang Mianxue, Zhu Qiming, Ke Hua, Liu Jiadong, Gao Aiting, Yu Jianting, Ni Ming, Chen Hao, Wang Ruolin, Wei Lian'i.

第十部分

老 之 将 至

年届九十的黄华虽然思想敏捷，书写流畅，生活有序，但总是精力有限。他几年前提出来，请年轻的和德才兼优的同志来担任五组织的领导工作。这一愿望已多半实现。

2002 年 11 月，黄华荣幸地作为特邀代表出席了党的第十六次全国代表大会。

黄华一生好读书，退休下来，正好多读些书，补自己之缺漏，真是得其所哉。

退休后的黄华有更多的时间会会朋友，参加各种社会活动，同老伴何理良和儿孙们谈笑。他喜爱钓鱼、摄影、看球赛、听戏、抚爱小动物。一贯关心国内的发展和国际形势，天天上网。

黄华常用中国古文学著作中的字句"厚德载物，自强不息"来勉励自己。

Part Ten

Coming to Old Age

90-year-old Huang Hua, though still with an agile mind, writes with ease and smoothness and lives in an orderly way, yet is limited in energy. Several years ago, he suggested that young persons having both ability and integrity should replace him to lead the five non-governmental organizations. His wish generally has come true.

Huang Hua was honored to attend the 16th National Congress of CPC as a specially invited delegate in November 2002.

Huang Hua loves reading. Now after retirement he has more time to read so as to make up what he missed. It is indeed what he desired.

After retirement, Huang Hua has more time to meet friends, participate in social activities, chat and laugh with He Liliang and offsprings. He loves fishing, photographing, watching matches, listening to operas, caressing pets. He always concerns himself with the development of the internal and international affairs, keeps up with the current situation and logs onto the internet daily.

He often spurs himself with the celebrated dictum from the Chinese classics: "Carry weight with great virtue, strengthen oneself without letup."

X-1 1999年9月30日，在国庆五十周年宴会上，同习仲勋同志向江泽民主席祝酒。左一为黄华。

September 30, 1999. Together with Comrade Xi Zhongxun(center) Huang Hua greets President Jiang Zemin at the banquet to celebrate the 50th anniversary of the founding of the People's Republic of China. First left: Huang Hua.

X-2　1996年9月，同老红军合影。前排左三为张爱萍，左四为黄华,左五为李德生，右二为王定国。
September 1996. With veterans of the Red Army.Third left in front row:Zhang Aiping,fourth left: Huang Hua,fifth left: Li Desheng,second right :Wang Dingguo.

X-3　1977年3月，看望朱德夫人康克清。
March 1977. Visiting Kang Keqing, wife of Zhu De.

X-4　1982年夏，看望叶剑英委员长。
Summer 1982. Visiting Ye Jianying, Chairman of the Standing Committee of the National People's Congress.

X-5　1997年夏，看望九十岁高龄的杨尚昆。左一为世界华人摄影学会会长杨绍明。
Summer 1997. Visiting 90-year-old Yang Shangkun. First left: Yang Shaoming, Chairman of the World Overseas Chinese Photographers' Association.

X-6　2002 年 11 月，在中共十六大上，同前政治局常委宋平同志合影。 *王新庆摄。*
November 2002. With Song Ping, a former member of Standing Committee of Political Bureau of CPC Central
Committee, at the 16th National Congress of CPC. *Photo by Wang Xinqing.*

X-7 1987 年春，同维吾尔族老革命家、全国人大常委会副委员长赛福鼎·艾则孜亲切交谈。
Spring 1987. A cordial chat with Syfiddin Azizi, a veteran revolutionist of Uygur nationality, Vice Chairman of the Standing Committee of the National People's Congress.

X-8 1983 年 7 月，同对西藏的解放作出杰出贡献的全国人大副委员长阿沛·阿旺晋美在浙江省海宁合影。
July 1983. With Ngapo Ngawang Jigme, Vice Chairman of the Standing Committee of the National People's Congress, who made outstanding contribution to the liberation of Tibet. Photo taken at Haining County of Zhejiang Province.

X-9　2003年1月，同广东省委书记张德江合影。
January 2003. With Zhang Dejiang, Secretary of the Provincial Party Committee of Guangdong Province.

X-10　同中国国际友人研究会副会长暨北京医院名誉院长、老朋友吴蔚然大夫合影。
With good friend Dr. Wu Weiran, Vice-President of PFS and honorary director of Beijing Hospital.

X-11　1996年6月，在华君武漫画展上同中国美协副主席华君武、李政道和赵毅敏合影。华君武于1938年读了埃德加·斯诺的《西行漫记》后奔赴延安，投身革命。华君武是本画册封面书法作者。自左至右：华君武、李政道、黄华、赵毅敏。

June 1996. With Hua Junwu, Vice Chairman of the Chinese Artists' Association, Professor T. D. Lee and Zhao Yimin at Hua Junwu's caricature exhibition. Hua Junwu went to Yan'an to join the revolution in 1938 after reading Edgar Snow's *Red Star over China*. He writes the cover calligraphy of this pictorial album. From left: Hua Junwu, Professor T. D. Lee, Huang Hua, Zhao Yimin.

X-12　1995年6月,同沙博理亲切交谈。沙博理原为美国律师,四十年代来华,1963年加入中国籍,长期从事中国文学审译工作。1983年至今为全国政协委员,是宋庆龄基金会和中国国际友人研究会的资深理事,是本画册的英文总审编。

June 1995. A cordial chat with Sydney Shapiro, who was an American lawyer, came to China in the 1940s, became a Chinese citizen in 1963. He has translated many Chinese literary works. A member of the National Committee of CPPCC since 1983 and a senior council member of Soong Ching Ling Foundation and PFS, he is English consultant of this pictorial album.

X-13　1998 年秋，同著名美国问题专家、中国社会科学院美国研究所所长资中筠合影。
Autumn 1998. With Zi Zhongyun, a scholar of American studies and Director of American Research Institute, China Academy of Social Sciences.

X-14　2001 年 9 月，同原体改委副主任和美国斯诺纪念基金会访问教授高尚全合影。
September 2001. With Professor Gao Shangquan, former Vice-Minister of State Commission for
Economic Restructuring and visiting professor of U.S. Edgar Snow Memorial Fund.

X-15

X-16

X-15 中国国际友人研究会的上上下下都是以奉献为乐的热情家。左二为新会长凌青。

All the staff of the China Society for People's Friendship Studies are enthusiasts ready to make contribution. Second left: Ling Qing, newly elected President.

X-16 1997年3月,同友联会副会长李长顺一同访问印度。

March 1997. With Li Changshun, Vice Chairman of China Association for International Friendly Contact, on a visit to India.

X–17　1998年夏，在美国普林斯顿大学校园内，同知名经济学教授邹至庄和夫人陈国瑞合影。
Summer 1998. With Gregory Chow, a well-known professor of economics, Princeton University, and Mrs. Paula Chow in Princeton campus, U.S.A.

X–18　1996年春，在北京同中国人民的老朋友、联合国儿童基金会执行主任詹姆士·格兰特见面。正中为河北衡水哈里逊纪念医院的陈院长。
Spring 1996. Meeting with James Grant, an old friend of Chinese people and Executive Director of UNICEF in Beijing. Center: Director Chen of Harrison Memorial Hospital in Hengshui.

X–17

X–18

X-19　2001年9月，在北京医院病房内会见美国前国务卿亚历山大·黑格将军。

September 2001. Receiving General Alexander Haig, former U.S. Secretary of State, in Huang Hua's ward, Beijing Hospital.

X-21　2002年7月，同加拿大驻华大使柯杰合影。

July 2002. With Joseph Caron, Canadian Ambassador to China.

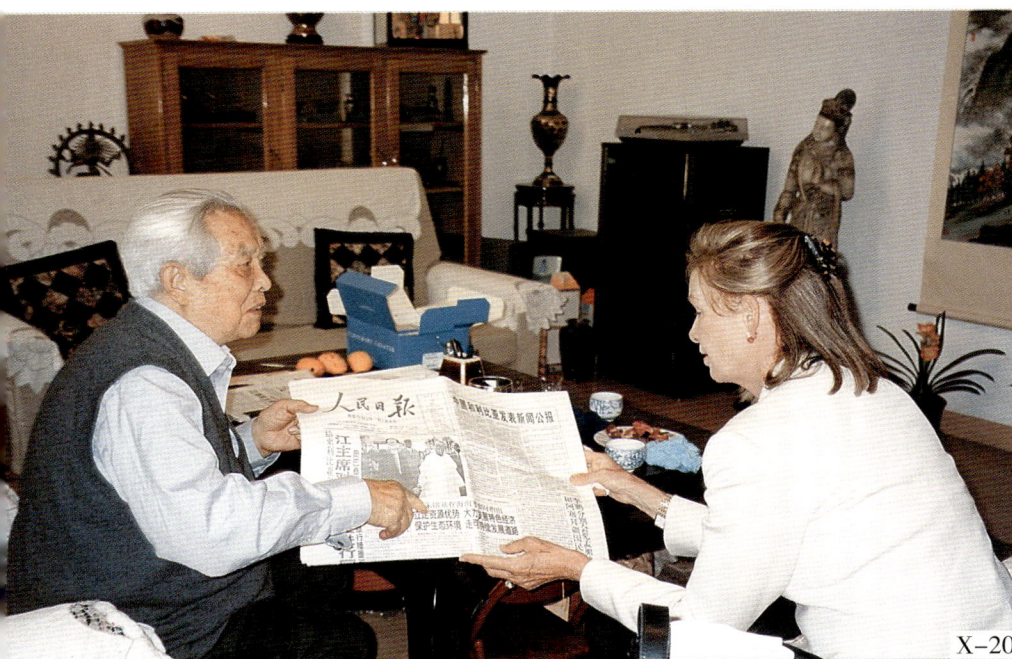

X-20　2000年秋，同英国作家、好友奥利维亚合影。

Autumn 2000. With good friend Olivia Cox-Fill, a British writer.

X-22　1990年春，同马海德之子、出色的摄影家周幼马合影。

Spring 1990. With Zhou Youma, son of Dr. George Hatem and an excellent photograhper.

X-23　1989年10月，在奥地利瓦滕斯城，同奥地利友人格尔诺·兰格斯－斯华洛奇合影。

October 1989. With Austrian friend Gernot Langes-Swarovski in Wattens City, Austria.

X-24　1995年夏，同美国友人有吉辛治之子罗杰·有吉在北京合影。

Summer 1995. With Roger Ariyoshi, son of Koji Ariyoshi ,an old friend of China,in Beijing.

X-25 2002 年 11 月，作为特邀代表出席中共第十六次全国代表大会。
November 2002. Attending the 16th National Congress of CPC as a specially invited delegate.

X-25

X-26 1987 年春，同革命老同志曹瑛和陈维清合影。
Spring 1987. With Comrades-in-arms Cao Ying and Chen Weiqing.

X-26

X-27 在书房中。
In the study.

X-28 天天上网。*杨绍明摄。*
Surfing the internet daily. *Photo by Yang Shaoming.*

X-29 同年轻有为的企业家、瑞得集团董事长钱英洪合影。
With Qian Yinghong, a successful young industrialist and President of READ Group.

X-30　1999年3月，黄华同著名考古学家、陕西考古研究所所长韩伟合影。
March 1999. With Han Wei, a famous archaeologist and Director of Shaanxi Archaeological Institute.

X-31　四代同堂。自左至右：黄玫、黄华、珊珊、王艾英、何理良。1986年3月摄于北京。
Four generations under one roof. From left: Huang Mei, Huang Hua, Shanshan, Wang Aiying, He Liliang. Photo taken in March 1986 in Beijing.

X-32 欢迎荻笛加入我们的家庭。1998年12月摄。
Welcoming Dede to join our family. Photo taken in December 1998.

X-33 我们特喜欢爷爷。2004年1月摄于深圳。
We particularly love Grandpa. Photo taken in January 2004 in Shenzhen.

X–34 爱好摄影。
Taking pictures is a hobby.

X–35 喜看手栽的幼树茁壮挺秀。2003年2月在深圳仙湖同黄玫、曹一珊和曹吉东合影。
February 2003. Happy to see the young tree planted by Huang Hua grow sturdy and strong. Photo taken at Xianhu Lake in Shenzhen with Huang Mei, Cao Yishan and Cao Jidong.

X-36　喜欢犬类，它们是人类的朋友和助手。
Love for dogs—friends and assistants of human beings.

X-37　湖光塔影忆华年。
Thoughts are far beyond the lake and pagoda of the Yenching compound.

X-36

X-37

X-38 从今天起步入九十岁的阶段。
A young age of 90 today.

X-39 回首往事，更觉祖国前景美好。
Recalling the past, one even feels the motherland will have a bright future.

X-40　九十华诞的黄爷爷属鼠，中国福利会的小朋友专门设计和制作剪纸，祝他健康长寿。

90-year-old grandpa Huang Hua was born in the year of the rat. Little friends from China Welfare Institute specially design and make the paper-cut, wishing him good health and long life.

X-41　2003年9月，宋庆龄基金会、中国福利会、中国国际友好联络会、中国国际友人研究会等举行中秋联谊会，并庆祝《黄华》画册出版。图为胡启立、荣高棠、阿依木·艾则孜、宋平、黄华、吴阶平、伍沾德同切喜糕。

September 11, 2003, six organizations including Soong Ching Ling Foundation, China Welfare Institute, China Association for International Friendly Contact, and China Society for People's Friendship Studies celebrated the Mid-Autumn Festival at the Great Wall Hotel. From left to right : Hu QiLi, Rong Gaotang, Aimu Azezi, Song Ping, Huang Hua, Wu Jieping, James T. Wu.

X-42 相伴不觉近六旬。*鲁明摄。*

Nearly 60 years of marriage have slipped by. *Photo by Lu Ming.*

后　记

　　由中国福利会、中国宋庆龄基金会、中国国际友好联络会、中国国际友人研究会和中国长城学会等五个非政府组织倡议的《黄华》画册在各位顾问和特约编委的大力支持和指导下编辑工作已告完成。

　　我们衷心感谢宋平同志和凌青同志在百忙中写了前言和序言，以及不顾大手术后的虚弱和行动不便而热情书写了贺信的长者爱泼斯坦同志。华君武同志题写书名给画册带来了活泼和生气。

　　我们十分感激外交部、全国人大常委、中央文献研究室、新华通讯社新闻摄影部、中国照片档案馆、人民日报社、北京市档案馆、许多新老战友、摄影专家、外国驻华大使馆、海外朋友的热情关怀和帮助。

　　这部画册得到上述五组织的鼎力赞助和伍沾德、宋志平、钱英洪、荻笛、刘军、黄峥等朋友的热情支援，画册的顺利出版是同他们的贡献分不开的。

　　此画册编辑之时，喜逢党的第十六次全国代表大会召开。作为一个老党员，黄华看到中国社会主义事业在党的三代领导集体的指引下发展兴盛，感到振奋万分。黄老时刻惦念和希望的是在中国共产党的领导下，在千百万党团员和亿万各族人民的不懈努力下，我国必将成为更加繁荣、民主和文明的社会主义国家。他坚信，中国的前途无限光明。

何理良

2002 年 12 月

《黄华》画册第二版说明

　　《黄华》画册出版发行后受到广大读者的欢迎，许多朋友觉得应该再版，供更多的中外人士阅读。第二版保留了绝大部分原用照片，增加了一些过去未及收入和近期的照片，希望读者喜欢。

何理良

2006 年 9 月

Epilogue

We have finished with the compilation of the pictorical album HUANG HUA, proposed by the five NGOs, namely the China Welfare Institute, the Soong Ching Ling Foundation, the China Association for International Friendly Contact, the China Society for People's Friendship Studies and the China Great Wall Society, together with the energetic support and guidance of the advisors and special editorial members.

We wish to express our heartfelt thanks to comrades Song Ping and Ling Qing, who in the midst of pressing affairs, managed to find time to write the FOREWORD and PREFACE respectively, and also to comrade Israel Epstein, who in his late eighties, despite debility and difficulty in getting about after a major operation, sent his ebullient greetings. The cover calligaphy by comrade Hua Junwu has added liveliness and vitality to the album.

We are grateful for the enthusiastic concern shown and help given by the Ministry of Foreign Affairs, the Standing Committee of the National People's Congress, the Department for the Research on Party Literature of the Central Committee of the Communist Party of China, the News Photography Department of Xinhua News Agency, the China Photo Archives, the People's Daily and Beijing Archives as well as many comrades-in-arms, old and new, professional photographers, foreign embassies in Beijing and overseas friends.

The successful publication of the album, which the above-mentioned five NGOs spared no effort to sponsor and was warmly supported by friends like James T.Wu, Song Zhiping, Qian Yinghong, Dede, Liu Jun, Huang Zheng and others, is inseparable from their contributions.

Preparation of the album happily coincided with the opening of the 16th National Congress of the Communist Party of China. As an old Party member, Huang Hua is greatly inspired by the flourishing development of China's socialist cause under the guidance of the Party's leading collective of three generations. It is Huang Hua's dearest hope and expectation that under the leadership of the Communist Party of China and with unremitting efforts made by all the Party members and hundreds of millions of people of all nationalities, China will become a more prosperous, democratic and civilized socialist country. Huang Hua firmly believes that China has a brilliant future.

He Liliang
December 2002

Note to the pictorial album HUANG HUA-Edition II

The publishing of the pictorial album HUANG HUA was welcomed throughout China with a high demand for republishing of the album.HUANG HUA-Edition II keeps most of the pictures shown in the previous edition. It also included pictures that were not added in the past and pictures that were taken recently. We hope you enjoy reading this edition of the pictorial album HUANG HUA.

He Liliang
Septemper 2006

黄华简历

　　1913年1月出生于河北省磁县，原名王汝梅。1932年秋至1936年夏在燕京大学读书，参加1935年12月9日的学生抗日救亡运动。1936年1月加入中国共产党。同年6月，随埃德加·斯诺赴陕北苏区采访担任翻译。9月，参加中国红军。1941年6月，任八路军总司令朱德的政治秘书。1944年7月任延安中共中央军事委员会外事组翻译科长，负责同美军驻延安观察组的联络工作。1946年1月任中共方面驻北平军事调处执行部的新闻处处长。1949年1月至1953年10月先后任天津市、南京市、上海市军事管制委员会的外事处处长。1954年4月任中国出席日内瓦会议代表团的顾问和发言人。1955年5月任中国出席万隆会议的顾问和发言人。1960年7月至1971年11月，先后任中国驻加纳、埃及和加拿大大使。1971年7月，作为中央三人小组成员协助周恩来总理同秘密访华的美国总统安全助理基辛格博士谈判关于邀请尼克松总统访华的公告。1971年11月任中国出席第二十六届联合国大会代表团副团长和常驻联合国与安理会代表。1976年12月任外交部长。

　　1983年6月当选为第六届全国人大常委会副委员长。1973年、1977年和1982年当选为中共第十、十一、十二届中央委员。1987年10月当选为中共中央顾问委员会常务委员。1984年4月以来先后担任五个非政府组织的主席。

Huang Hua's Resume

Huang Hua was born in Cixian, Hebei Province in January 1913, originally named Wang Rumei, studied at Yenching University from Autumn 1932 to Summer 1936, participated in December 9th 1935 student movement of resistance against Japan and national salvation, joined the Communist Party of China in January 1936, accompanied the American journalist Edgar Snow as interpreter to visit the Soviet Region in the Northern Shaanxi Province in June in the same year. Huang Hua joined the Red Army in September . In June 1941, he worked as Political Secretary for Zhu De, Commander-in-chief of the 8th Route Army. In July 1944, he was the head of the Translation Section of the Foreign Affairs Office, the Military Committee of CPC, worked with the U.S.Army Observer Group in Yenan. In January 1946, he was Director of Information, Peking Military Executive Headquarters of the CPC Side.

From January 1949 to October 1953, he was successively the Director of Foreign Affairs Office of the Military Control Commission in Tianjing, Nanjing and Shanghai. In April 1954, he was Adviser and Spokesman of the Chinese delegation to the Geneva Conference. In May 1955, he was Adviser and Spokesman of the Chinese delegation to the Bandong Conference. From July 1960 to November 1971 he was successively appointed Ambassador to Ghana, Egypt and Canada. In July 1971, as a member of the 3-Persons Group, he assisted Premier Zhou Enlai in negotiations with Dr. Kissinger, National Security Assistant to U.S. President, on the announcement of inviting U.S. President Nixon to visit China. In November 1971, he was appointed Deputy Head of the Chinese delegation to the 26th United Nations General Assembly, Permanent Representative to the United Nations and its Security Council. Huang Hua was appointed Minister of Foreign Affairs in December 1976.

In June 1983, he was elected Vice-Chairman of the Standing Committee of 6th National People's Congress, led delegations to visit seven countries in Africa and Latin America, elected member of the 10th, 11th and 12th Central Committee of CPC in 1973, 1977 and 1982. In October 1987, he was elected member of the Standing Committee of the Advisory Committee of CPC. Since April 1984, he was the Chairman of 5 Non-Government Organizations: China Welfare Institute, China Soong Ching Ling Foundation, China Association for Friendly Contact, China Society for People's Friendship Studies and Great Wall Society of China.

顾 问

宋 平　　雷洁琼（女）　　吴阶平　　邹家骅　　宋 健　　叶选平

胡启立　　汪道涵　　荣高棠　　唐家璇　　朱穆之　　逄先知

李肇星　　侯仁之　　宋 黎　　李 昌　　韩天石　　爱泼斯坦

特约编委 （以姓氏笔画为序）

于光远　　王仲芳　　王定国（女）王光亚　　王效贤（女）王 毅　　邓朴方

朱 敏（女）华君武　　李凤林　　李长顺　　李储文　　伍沾德　　庄 焰

刘 英（女）刘 军　　吴 青（女）吴蔚然　　苏 菲（女）汪 溪（女）许德馨（女）

沙博理　　宋志平　　余建亭　　尚 明　　周 南　　周幼马　　陆 璀（女）

邵华泽　　杨绍明　　杨洁篪　　陈秀霞（女）柯 华　　张德华（女）张 振

赵惠中　　俞贵麟　　柴泽民　　梁 湜　　梁于藩　　高 梁　　凌 青

姜恩柱　　钱永年　　钱英洪　　钱嗣杰　　资中筠（女）浦寿昌　　徐肖冰

徐晓东　　崔天凯　　廉正保　　黄 玫（女）黄祖安　　龚普生（女）舒 元

鲁 平　　熊向晖　　廖心文（女）潘开文　　冀朝铸

法律顾问

黄嘉华　　任继圣

主编　副主编

何理良　　李长顺　俞贵麟　许德馨　凌 青　舒 暲　顾品锷　董耀会

英文总审编　英文编审

沙博理　　俞志忠　　舒 暲　　顾品锷

图书在版编目（CIP）数据

黄华／何理良主编.—北京：中国和平出版社，2003.4
（2007.7 重印）
ISBN 978-7-80154-713-2

Ⅰ.黄... Ⅱ.何... Ⅲ.黄华—生平事迹—摄影集Ⅳ.
K827=7

中国版本图书馆 CIP 数据核字（2003）第 024969 号

责任编辑／王晓晴
　　　　　任梦熊
文字责编／陈晓秋
美术责编／杨　隽
责任校对／邸　洁
　　　　　毛术芳
监　印／王　红
　　　　宋小仓

黄　华

何理良　主编
※
中国和平出版社出版发行
北京市西城区鼓楼西大街 154 号 100009
电话：(010)84026164　84026019
※
新华书店经销
※
深圳中华商务联合印刷有限公司制版印刷
电话：(0755)2845-8333　邮政编码：518111
※
889mm × 1194mm　1/16　14.25 印张　印数:4001–6000 册
2007 年 7 月第 2 版 2007 年 7 月第 1 次印刷
ISBN 978−7−80154−713−2/D・4
定价：148.00 元

Pictorial Album　HUANG HUA
Chief Editor：He Liliang
Published by China Peace Publishing House
154 Gulou West Street, Beijing
Tel：(010)8402-6161　8402-6019　Zip Code: 100009
Distributed by Xinhua Book Store
Printed by Shenzhen C & C Joint Printing Co.Ltd.
Tel:(0755)2845-8333　Zip Code: 518111
889mm × 1194mm　1/16　14.25　4000 copies
First Edition：August 2003
ISBN 978−7−80154−713−2/D・4
Price：RMB 148 yuan